Rooted in Grace

Missional Wisdom Foundation Titles for Christian Community:

Larry Duggins
- *A Man's Field Guide to Prayer: Discovering and Developing This Ancient Practice* (Introduction)
- *Clarify for College Ministries*, (Editor)
- *Feasting on the Gospels, Luke Vol. 1* (Contributor)
- *Missional. Monastic. Mainline: A Guide to Starting Missional Micro-Communities in Historically Mainline Traditions* (Co-authored with Elaine Heath)
- *Simple Harmony: Thoughts on Holistic Christian Life*
- *Together: Community as a Means of Grace*

Elaine Heath
- *Abide: A Guide to Living in Intentional Community* (Editor)
- *Five Means of Grace: Experience God's Love the Wesleyan Way*
- *God Unbound: Wisdom for Galatians for the Anxious Church*
- *The Gospel According to Twilight: Women, Sex, and God*
- *Longing for Spring: A New Vision for Wesleyan Community*
- *Missional. Monastic. Mainline: A Guide to Starting Missional Micro-Communities in Historically Mainline*

Traditions (Co-authored with Larry Duggins)

- *More Light on the Path: Daily Scripture Readings in Hebrew and Greek*
- *The Mystic Way of Evangelism: A Contemplative Vision for Christian Outreach*
- *Naked Faith: The Mystical Theology of Phoebe Palmer*
- *We Were the Least of These: Reading the Bible with Survivors of Sexual Abuse*

Bret Wells

- *What Kind of God?: Reading the Bible with a Missional Church*
- *Abide: A Guide to Living in Intentional Community. Contributor*
- "Helping the Church Be the Church: The Contribution of the New Monasticism," in Catalyst: Contemporary Evangelical Perspectives for United Methodist Seminarians, February 2012

Andrea Lingle

- *Credulous: A Journey Through Life, Faith, and the Bulletin*

Justin Hancock

- *The Julian Way: A Theology of Fullness for All God's People*

Wendy Miller

- *Come With Me: Daily Living with a New Monastic Rule of Life*
- *Jesus, Our Spiritual Director: A Pilgrimage Through the Gospels*

Rooted in Grace

Essays on Dialogue Without Division

Larry Duggins

Andrea L. Lingle,

Editors

 COLUMKILLE Press • Southlake, Texas

ROOTED IN GRACE
Essays on Dialogue Without Division

Columkille Press
185 S. White Chapel Rd.
Southlake, TX 76092

www.missionalwisdom.com

PAPERBACK ISBN: 978-1724524089

Cover Design and line drawing by Wendi Bernau
Table Blessings by Stephanie Evelyn McKellar
Words of Benediction by Rose Oxley
Liturgies by Andrea L. Lingle unless noted

Cataloguing-in-Pulication data:

Names: Duggins, Larry and Andrea L. Lingle, editors

Title: Rooted in Grace: essays on dialogue without division / Larry Duggins and Andrea L. Lingle.

Description: Southlake, TX: Columkille Press, 2018 | Includes bibliographical references.

Indentifiers: ISBN 978-1724524089 (paperback)

Classification: 978-1724524089 2018 (print)

Manufactured in the U.S.A.   08/01/18

CONTRIBUTORS

In order of appearance:

Dr. Larry Duggins is the co-founder, Executive Director, and a Leader of the Missional Wisdom Foundation. His most recent book is *Together: Community as a Means of* Grace (Cascade, 2017). Larry is an elder in full connection in the Central Texas Conference of the United Methodist Church.

Andrea L. Lingle serves as Editor, Staff Writer, and Lay Theologian of the Missional Wisdom Foundation. She is the author of *Credulous: A Journey Through Life, Faith, and the Bulletin* (Cascade, 2018).

Rev. Luke Lingle serves as a Leader of the Missional Wisdom Foundation. Luke has served in the local church and on conference staff within the Western North Carolina Conference, where he is an elder in full connection.

Denise Crane serves as a Leader of the Missional Wisdom Foundation. Following a career as a senior executive in the telecommunications industry, Denise became a trained spiritual director and has honed her gift of spiritual listening. She is a contributing writer to *What Kind of God?: Reading the Bible with a Missional Church* (Cascade, 2018).

Dr. Bret Wells serves a Leader of the Missional Wisdom Foundation. Bret has served a church planter in the Church of Christ, is an ICF Certified Professional Coach, and an expert in distance learning and evaluation. He is the author of *What Kind of God?: Reading the Bible with a Missional Church* (Cascade, 2018).

Rev. Stephanie Evelyn McKellar serves as a Writer and Community Pastor for the Missional Wisdom Foundation. She is a co-author of *The Project Transformation Guidebook* (2018), a curriculum guide developed in cooperation with Project Transformation. At the time of this writing, Evey is a provisional deacon in the Central Texas Conference of the United Methodist Church.

Rev. Wendi Bernau serves as Pastor for the Arts for the Missional Wisdom Foundation. She is a co-author of *The Project Transformation Guidebook* (2018), a curriculum guide developed in cooperation with Project Transformation. At the time of this writing, Wendi is a provisional deacon in the Central Texas Conference of the United Methodist Church.

Rev. Kathryn Hunter is a retired elder from the South Carolina Conference of the United Methodist Church. In 2018, Kathryn and her husband Jim traveled with the Missional Wisdom Foundation on pilgrimage to Iona, Scotland.

Robert L. Bishop serves as the Director of Learning Strategy for the Missional Wisdom Foundation. Robert is a distance learning and curriculum design expert and is an ICF certified coach.

Rev. Justin Hancock is co-founder of the Julian Way and the Prior of the Epworth Project for the Missional Wisdom Foundation. His most recent book is *The Julian Way: A Theology of*

Fullness for All God's People (Cascade, 2018). Justin is a deacon in full connection in the North Texas Conference of the United Methodist Church.

Lisa Hancock is co-founder of the Julian Way and lives in community at The Cochran House, a part of the Missional Wisdom Foundation's Epworth Project. Lisa is a Ph.D. candidate working in disability theology at Southern Methodist University.

Taylor Pryde serves as an intern at Haw Creek Commons, a project of the Missional Wisdom Foundation. At the time of this writing, Taylor is a candidate for a Master of Divinity at Duke Divinity School and a certified candidate for elder in the Michigan Conference.

Ryan Klinck serves as a Spiritual Director for the Missional Wisdom Foundation. He has organized and led new monastic communities in the Epworth Project, and is currently working with the Neighboring Movement / SoceLife team to develop curriculum and more deeply incorporate the work of community development into the teachings of the MWF.

Rose Oxley lives in community within the Epworth Project of the Missional Wisdom Foundation. At the time of this writing, Rose is a candidate for a Master of Divinity at Perkins School of Theology and a certified candidate for elder in the Mountain Sky Conference of the United Methodist Church.

Katey Rudd is the Cultivator at Haw Creek Commons, a project of the Missional Wisdom Foundation. Her primary role is to cultivate community, gardens, and coworking and maker spaces where residents of the Haw Creek community can gather and grow. Katey is a Registered Dietitian and an integrative health coach.

Rev. Sarah Howell-Miller is the Prioress of The Foundry House, an intentional community on the campus of Crossnore School & Children's Home in Winston-Salem, where she serves under appointment to the Missional Wisdom Foundation. Sarah is an elder in full connection in the Western North Carolina Conference of the United Methodist Church.

Rev. Darryl Dayson, II serves as Associate Pastor for Trinity UMC and Senior Pastor at Berry Temple UMC in Asheville, NC. He is currently a student in the Missional Wisdom Foundation's Launch & Lead program. He is an elder in full connection in the Western North Carolina Conference of the United Methodist Church.

"I ask not only on behalf of these, but also on behalf of those who will believe in me through their word, that they may all be one. As you, Father, are in me and I am in you, may they also be in us, so that the world may believe that you have sent me."

John 17:20, 21

Table of Contents

Introduction

BY: LARRY DUGGINS

EVERY TIME I TURN on the television, I seem to be confronted by people arguing. Many of the major news outlets have hired teams of "analysts" whose job it is to reflect the extreme positions of political parties in an entirely disagreeable and, apparently, entertaining manner. The politicians themselves are not much better, with many resorting to name calling or personal attacks to appeal to their political base. It seems rare to encounter a discussion where two parties who disagree with one another simply discuss the issue in a civil and polite way.

Unfortunately, this form of discourse has taken root in normal, everyday discussions. Social media allows the ability to respond instantaneously before the filters of polite conversation can engage. We electronically shout at each other, knowing that our brilliant and pithy remarks will somehow change the mind of the world, or at least the mind of the person who wrote the initial post. We hide behind keyboards, not looking the person we are criticizing in the eye and pass judgment about whether that person is good or evil.

What are we teaching our kids and grandkids?

Introduction

At the time I am writing this, the United Methodist Church is engaged in such a discussion. After forty years of kicking the can forward, the issue of human sexuality is front and center. Is homosexual behavior sinful? Can LGBTQAI+ people be ordained? How do we read our Bibles? The Commission on a Way Forward was proposed by the Council of Bishops and approved by the 2016 General Conference to do a complete examination and possible revision of every paragraph of the Book of Discipline concerning human sexuality and to explore options that help to maintain and strengthen the unity of the church. The Commission identified three possible plans for moving forward. The Council of Bishops voted to share the work done by the Commission on a Way Forward on the three plans and to recommend the One Church Plan. The One Church Plan will be placed before the specially called 2019 General Conference for legislative action.

And people are taking sides. Large groups are forming within the clergy and the laity to raise money and stake out positions. Individual annual conferences are receiving motions and resolutions designed to support one position or another. The rumor mill runs rampant with accusations and innuendos about the "other" group.

Yet another thing is happening too. Groups of faithful Methodists are gathering to discuss the issues around A Way Forward, and to try to prayerfully discern the direction that God is calling them. They seem to realize that something greater is at stake—that our very connection as the church and as the Body of Christ can be ripped apart unless we learn to listen without demonizing, to consider without denigrating, and to disagree without departing. That's where this book comes in.

Jesus was not bashful about sharing his opinions. He engaged in seemingly uncomfortable dialogues with common folk and with people in authority. One such discussion challenged the thought process of a powerful Pharisee (John 3) while another resulted in the transformation of a common woman at a well into the first evangelist (John 4). Jesus even occasionally lapsed into name-calling (Luke 13:32)! However, the goal of Jesus was always clear—to bring people into closer connection with God and with each other. He was about removing obstacles, freeing up choices, and helping people see a clearer path to God. And he was not above having his mind changed by a convincing argument (Mark 7:26–30)—he was an excellent listener.

So how can we follow this example of Jesus? Is it possible to have deep and important discussions without lapsing into rancor? Is it okay to be convinced? Is it okay to stay in community with those who believe differently than we?

The Missional Wisdom Foundation (MWF) experiments with and teaches about alternative forms of Christian community all over the United States. Over the past eight years, we have formed residential communities where people live together under a rule of life, home churches for refugees and people experiencing poverty, coworking spaces, beekeeping clubs, and literally dozens of other communities where people interact. That means we have done our fair share of mediating disputes, negotiating hard issues and making hard decisions. Yet, we are still together—still working on loving God and loving people in the world.

For that reason, we have invited a variety of people associated with the MWF to contribute essays on making hard discussions and staying in community with each other. These essays and exercises cover a wide variety of scripture, history, and perspectives, all tied to the idea of respectful listening and speaking. It is our hope that these essays will be a good starting point for folks to practice looking at hard issues together without requiring absolute conformity as a condition of belonging. Perhaps you will do this in the context of considering the Way Forward options, or maybe you simply want to explore the possibility of problem solving without animosity around any of the big issues our world faces today. It is our prayer that you can do so in such a way that strengthens your bond with God and with each other.

For those of you working on the Way Forward issues, please know that this book does not address the issues around human sexuality. We went in search of a good book that fairly deals with the various arguments around human sexuality and came upon *Two Views on Homosexuality, the Bible and the Church* (Zondervan, 2016). This wonderful book places four theologians into conversation—each of the four have individually written books on the topic. Four positions, two "affirming" and two "traditional," three men and one woman, and one gay person. Each author presents an argument, then each of the other three writes a response, and the cycle closes with a rejoinder by the original author. Almost as importantly as the subject analysis, the discussion is civil and respectful—each author is there to learn and to test. This book touches on tradition around marriage, on scriptural interpretation, on the role of culture in reading scripture, on celibacy, and on almost every other argument on the topic. It is a book written for adults—the authors are direct in their discussions of body parts and sex acts—which is refreshingly informative for the adult reader trying to form an opinion of their own.

We recommend *Two Views on Homosexuality, the Bible and the Church* for any group of adults trying to faithfully address the issues at the core of A Way Forward.

Finally, in a time of division, we wish you peace. May the Holy Spirit guide your inquiry and hold your tongue so that all may be heard, all may be appreciated, and all may draw closer to God and each other.

1

Preparing for Deep Conversation

BY: ANDREA LINGLE

YOUR HEART IS POUNDING. His face is flat, angry, and fixed. There is coffee in your cup, but it has gone cold. You sip at it anyway, just for something to do. You knew when the question was raised that there would be a fight. Now you are looking for a way out. Except. This thing. This question. This problem has already taken so many hours and so much joy—it is enough. Even though you find yourself shifting in your seat, you need to stay here, with him, with them. Because you made a commitment to walk this road with these people. But, how?

There are so many times in communities (of faith or otherwise) that conflict arises. In my house all it takes is for someone to cut up the watermelon wrong and I am gritting my teeth. People come into the world and our communities with preloaded assumptions, personalities, and systems of belief. The question that faces us and our communities of faith is: can we love people? And if so, how do we do so when communities encounter deep disagreement?

This book attempts to guide communities through a process of learning how to wade through conflict. Yes, conflict. Pretending that what we are experiencing when cherished doctrines are met with resistance isn't conflict keeps us from exercising the focused attention and care that conflict demands. Community is hard, but calls to humans on a fundamental, an elemental, level. So, if our communities are to survive conflict, what practices and tools will guide us?

The Missional Wisdom Foundation believes that there is a deep power in table fellowship. Christians began, not as people of the cross, but as people of the table. Before Jesus died, he demonstrated a practice of lovingly preparing and sharing a meal. Because the table represents humanity's universal need to be fed, to periodically ingest the power of another being (be that plant or animal), the table reminds us of our fundamental need for others. When Jesus broke bread, he instructed his disciples to break bread in remembrance of him—in remembrance of the life he lived in love of God, neighbor, and self. When we come to the table in the midst of turmoil and conflict, we are forced to encounter the other and the self. The clinking of spoons, the passing of salt, the submission to the mandate of hunger is a space of vulnerability, and when we are vulnerable with ourselves, does it not make us willing to see humanity in the other?

To connect the power of the table to our hope for fruitful dialog, this book has four liturgical chapters. Each chapter is designed to be used around a table with a group of people. Ideally, the group should be big enough to allow for interaction but small enough that no one gets forgotten in the corner or lost in the middle.

Each meeting begins with setting the table. Setting the table is an act of ridiculous hope. Hope that our needs will be met once again. Hope that she who is expected will arrive in time to participate. Hope that grace is found, already puddled up under this table on this day. So, there is liturgy for setting the table followed by a corporate blessing. All of the blessings coordinate with the four-part design of this book: Committing to Change,[1] Encountering the Other,[2] Encountering the Self,[3] and Committing to Grace.[4] This structure is important for teaching civil dialogue because it allows conflict to be encountered within growing relationship.

The corporate blessing is followed by the beginning of the meal. The passing of or by the food (family style or buffet), the coming to the prepared table, and the breaking of the bread are the beginnings of the mysterious work of loving someone completely other than yourself.

When the meal is underway, there are group practices provided to help build skills necessary for engaging in loving, fruitful, empathetic dialog. After the group practice, the participants are asked to discuss one of four essays that are included with each chapter. The group can pick one of the essays to read in preparation for the meal discussion or read the essay aloud at

1 Chapter 3

2 Chapter 4

3 Chapter 5

4 Chapter 6

the table. If the practice of eating and discussing is fruitful, the chapters can be used for four separate meals each focusing on a different essay. These essays do not introduce contentious issues, rather they are designed to give the participants practice discussing from a stance of holy listening and shared economy (see the essays at the end of this chapter).

After the meal, practice, and discussion are complete, there are instructions for mindfully cleaning up. Doing the dishes symbolizes that we are committing to maintaining this work beyond what happens in one encounter. Doing the dishes forces the participants to share a task even after possible disagreement. Doing the dishes is a commitment to the mundane work of bringing the Community of God to earth.

To help equip participant for this difficult and risky work, Chapters 1 and 2 give participants a very brief overview of why and how to design, enter, and inhabit spaces of conflict. The essays at the end of this chapter outline why people of faith should do this work ("The Implications of 'The Scripture Way of Salvation'" and "A Shared Economy") and how ("Holy Listening" and "When Things FAIL: What Coaching Teaches Us About Conflict"). Chapter 2 is a discussion of how to create a space that fosters both safety and bravery.

Welcome.

Thank you for committing to the work of embracing the grace present all around us and doing the hard, constant work of peace.

ESSAYS

The Implications of: "The Scripture Way of Salvation"

BY: LARRY DUGGINS

JOHN WESLEY MAY HAVE preached Ephesians 2:8, the scriptural foundation of his sermon "The Scripture Way of Salvation,"[5] more than any other text. According to Albert Outler,[6] Wesley preached this text around seventy times and returned to it several times as an organizing principle for other sermons and discussions. In the Common English Bible translation, the passage reads, "You are saved by God's grace because of your faith. This salvation is God's gift. It's not something you possessed."[7] Wesley's focus was simply the first sentence.

The sermon begins by proposing that most religion is too complicated, and that Christianity is very simple. The "ends" of Christianity is salvation, and the "means" of Christianity is faith. He explains that salvation is more than simply claiming the prize of heaven at the end of life and is, in fact, the present and immediate entire work of God. He defines faith as the evidence and conviction of things not seen. The sermon goes on to describe the flow of God's grace into the lives of people over their lifetime, and the

---

5 The complete sermon is available online at http://wesley.nnu.edu/john-wesley/the-sermons-of-john-wesley-1872-edition/sermon-43-the-scripture-way-of-salvation/.

6 This essay refers extensively to Albert Outler, ed., *The Works of John Wesley*, (Nashville: Abington Press, 1985).

7 *The Common English Study Bible.*

responses of people through faith that result in Christian growth. Through God's grace and responses of faith, people receive the gift of pardon and then continue to grow over time in faithful response to God's ongoing providence of grace in their lives.

Wesley's perception of the process of salvation and sanctification—an ongoing ballet of faithful human response to an uninterrupted stream of God's grace—is a very life-giving metaphor for me. I envision people doing their best to react to God's neverending grace, failing often, but, by God's grace, changing and growing in holiness over time. As people grow closer to God, their actions reflect their hearts, and, in turn, God's grace reaches even deeper into them through what Wesley calls the works of piety and the works of mercy. Good works further illuminate the goodness of God.

I am convinced that this metaphor holds much fruit for us as we consider our interactions with each other. The attitude of God, the role of human response, and the idea of growth all come into play.

This understanding of salvation is centered around a grace-filled God. From the earliest moment of life, God provides "prevenient" grace, or grace that comes before justification and the emergence of faith in a person. God acts first and God acts often, drawing people to God through invitation, not coercion. God does not wait for people to earn a place in God's presence and God does not require people to be in a sinless state to develop a faithful response. Rather, God invites and offers repeatedly until a person responds, and then God provides another invitation of grace allowing another human response to become possible, until God's grace and humanity's response yield the emergence of faith through faith, justification, and salvation. God does not break away from a person who does not respond. God offers again and again, allowing humanity chance after chance to respond in faith. God does not sever connections with those who sin and those who will not listen, God nudges over and over, inviting the emergence of faith.

Human response is also a critical component to this understanding of salvation. It takes people time to respond to God's grace. We read Luke 1 and marvel at the faithful response of Mary to the announcement from Gabriel that she is to be the mother of Jesus. We marvel because her response is so different than our own! I resonate much more with the response of Zechariah, who in that same story is struck dumb because he did not believe. Many of us must stand in the firehose of God's grace for a long time before we recognize that we might be getting wet. We struggle, we deny, we hold on to our egos, and we twist and turn before we finally acknowledge the presence and sovereignty of God in a way that allows faith to emerge.

But we can respond. Every one of us inherently has the capacity to embrace God's grace through faith. We will do so imperfectly, slowly, and in a manner that is completely devoid of any aspect of merit, but we can do so. And that is why God is persistent.

God's grace in the life of a person changes as the responses of faith change and grow over time. Sanctifying grace invites the faithful person to draw their will into alignment with the will of God. It helps people to increasingly set aside sin in their lives because the sovereignty of sin has been destroyed by the gift of salvation. God offers grace, and people respond to God through faith, and the person draws closer to God. Wesley encourages looking toward a state of entire sanctification, in which the will of the person and the will of God perfectly align. Over time, we work and we grow, not through our own merit, but through faithful response to God's grace.

To me, these three factors have very meaningful implications in considering conflict in Christian discourse. *First, we must be very patient.* God has every right to summarily discard people who do not respond to God's graceful nudges, yet God does not. Instead, God invites repeatedly, patiently staying connected to the reticent person offering invitation after invitation. God does not push away those who have not yet embraced faith.

Second, we must give people time to react. God understands that even after justification and new birth, people will fall short. Sin and repentance are part of the journey, and God expects and provides for that. God's grace flows as God's free gift, and does not depend on a person earning it in any way. It takes time to grow in holiness, and God expects mistakes, shortfalls, and errors in the process. It takes people time to resolve conflicts, and the process of resolution will be imperfect.

Finally, people will interact with each other at different points in their Christian journey. Growing in holiness takes time and requires faithful response, and people will move along that path of growth at different rates. It is possible that a person who has grown deeply in holiness might have a different perspective than one who has not yet walked that far. Just as God patiently walks with each of us at the point where we are, we must walk patiently with each other. We will all see through the glass darkly until we all walk to Christian perfection together. Until that time, our perspectives may be different.

Discussion questions:

- Is it helpful to you to envision your relationship with God as a path or a journey? Why or why not?
- Do you agree that the salvation metaphor John Wesley describes calls for us to be patient with each other?
- Do you feel that all people are capable of accepting God's offer of grace? Even people you don't like or disagree with?

A Shared Economy

BY: LUKE LINGLE

"Economics," according to Lionel Robbins, "is the study of the use of scarce resources which have alternative uses." [8]Thomas Sowell clarifies Robbins definition stating, "there has never been enough to satisfy everyone completely. That is the real constraint. That is what scarcity means."[9] It makes sense, if we look around us today, that an economist would posit that "what everybody wants adds up to more than there is."[10] However, my question is: What if what everybody needs is less than what is available? What if there is a way to order ourselves in such a way that what we need is potentially less than what we want?

The word "economy" comes from the Greek word *oikonomia*, which literally means house order. Quite simply, economics is the process of how we order ourselves as people. Don't believe this does not pertain to you; we are all a part of different economies. We are a part of economies in our families, with our friends, with groups we join, in our towns, states, country, and globally. We are participating in the economy and how the world around us is being ordered. The real question is are we participating intentionally in the economy or are we being ordered without recognizing our role in the ordering?

This begs the question for me, what if the work of economics has a connection to our theological work? What if our work

---

8 Sowell, *Basic Economics*, 2.

9 Sowell, *Basic Economics*, 3.

10 Sowell, *Basic Economics*, 3.

in community and with each other is both an exercise in how we order our lives together and how we understand the work of God in the world? Wendell Berry observes that our current economy, which is reflected in our local churches, is "based upon consumption, which ultimately serves, not the ordinary consumers, but a tiny class of excessively wealthy people for whose further enrichment the economy is understood (by them) to exist."[11] What if what we do in the church, what we are consuming today, exists for a select few who are inside, while not recognizing the needs of those outside of the church economy? Furthermore, what if our economy within the church is weaker because we need what folks outside of the church have to offer? How we order ourselves matters, and, if we order ourselves out of greed and consumption, then we create economies that do not value the needs of the community. If we order ourselves through a lens of power and seek our own wants over the needs of the other, then we are missing an opportunity to create, with God, a more robust economy.

In his book *The Wealth of Nations*, Adam Smith outlines the basic tenants of our modern economy. While Smith's is not the only voice that has shaped our modern economy, his is one of the most influential. Early in the book, Smith discusses the value of trade within the economy, explaining that a country that does not trade outside of itself is weaker than an country that trades with other countries. The idea behind this is that, if we trade, then every country does not have to produce everything that is needed for the local economy. Resources can be traded for or traded away depending on the needs of the economy.

---

11 Berry, *What Matters?*, 5.

What I have begun to wonder is, what if, as faith communities, we have created a closed economy? More precisely, what if our churches have created closed economies by not trading outside of themselves? What exactly would a church trade? Our churches have the opportunity to trade thoughts and ideas, to trade support and a listening ear, to trade hope and a word or love? What would we expect to receive in return? Nothing, the expectation is nothing, but the hope would be relationship, simply relationship. With relationship comes other aspects of a person's life, but it is no more or no less than the most valuable thing a person has to share. We have closed our economies by asking for more than we need from a person; the church has been asking for wants. We have become greedy and self-seeking, we have asked for what we want and have pushed passed our needs, believing that we have all the answers and that what we may learn through relationship in and of itself is less valuable than what we might gain from a relationship that fits our wants. What if we have more need than we realize, and by not having relationship with others our economy is less robust?

The church has become an economy that believes that we have all that we need, that we can supply for ourselves all that we need. In some sense that may seem like the best idea. We have all we need and we are not wanting more than we need. We are not consuming outside of what we can produce, and our needs are being met. But what if Adam Smith is correct, what if by participating in a closed economy we have created weaker entities of our local churches? What if the trade is not about consumption but is about intentional mutual sharing so that all might have enough? If an entity that does not trade outside of itself is weaker, then is it reasonable to say that when our churches practice closed economies they are not as robust as they could be. Furthermore, if a church is not as vibrant as it could be, then is it possible that our churches are made up of folks who have closed themselves off to the economy around them? And if we intentionally participate in the economy around us, then we have the opportunity learn from each other and share what we have learned in the process.

How do we reclaim our house order? One of the first steps is to recognize that everyone has something to offer the economy, and to affirm that we need each other in order to participate in a more robust economy. Another question to ask is, how do we value the needs of the community and order ourselves in such a way that all people are valued and that ideas outside of our experience are ideas that we value in trade? This last question is difficult. Sometimes we disagree with each other, we don't find value in what another person has to say or even agree with what is said, and we, at times, believe that if we trade for certain ideas we might be harmed. When we open our economies up for trade there is always the risk of being harmed, and I would never advocate for anyone to be put in a position to be hurt. However, when we open our economies up for trade there is the possibility for new relationship. We might hear or see something that is unexpected that, in the end, is exactly what we need.

Discussion questions:

- Do you believe that there is enough to supply everyone's need?
- What fears do you have about "trading" viewpoints and opinions outside the economy you are comfortable with?
- What is the risk involved? What is the benefit?

Holy Listening

BY: DENISE CRANE

WHAT DOES IT MEAN to be a holy listener? What does it mean to hold the center or create open space in difficult conversations or disagreements? Is it putting yourself between the "rock and the hard place?" And if so, must you just get squished by the opposing voices? Are you wishy-washy because you resist the urge to add your voice to those on either end? Are you the rope in a game of tug-of-war where each end wants to pull you to their side? What does it mean to hold holy space, and how do we do it well?

I would say that holy listening and holding open space requires a strength and focus that many will find hard to sustain. I have heard it described by friends of mine as creating a border-land where people can meet and talk but do not have to cross a border. In my moments of despairing over whether humans can be human to each other, I sometimes think of this space as a demili-tarized zone. It's hard space. It feels as if you cannot bandage all the wounds or properly honor all the real or metaphorical blood-shed. I recently had a young clergy person say to me that she is too conservative for her liberal friends and too liberal for her conser-vative friends. Ouch. How do we hold that? How do we recog-nize our own interior landscape well enough to really and truly let people say what they need to say, honor what they say, and respect them as equally beloved children of God?

To be like Switzerland, you have to create Switzerland first.

For me, this requires a contemplative stance. Several years ago I learned a four step litany that helps me frame this posture. Dr. Elaine Heath, former professor of Evangelism at Perkins School of Theology, now Dean of Duke Divinity School and co-founder of the Missional Wisdom Foundation puts it this way: Show up, pay attention, cooperate with God, release the outcome[12].

To show up in the context of holy listening means that we are fully present. We listen with intentionality, and we do it while holding hands with the Holy Spirit. There is a stance in holy listening. It is open and receiving and welcoming. You cannot hold it if you are watching your phone for a call, haven't lifted at least a breath prayer for guidance and wisdom, or are in turmoil about something else that you haven't been able to lay aside yet. Please, let us get ourselves ready for listening. If I am not ready, I postpone starting, as briefly as possible, to prepare my inner soil. Once I start listening, seeds are going to be planted all over that soil and I want to be prepared to tend them appropriately. I can trust God to do the weeding later that may need to be done, but I have to have a tending stance in order to listen effectively.

We pay attention, and in this holy listening context I believe that we have to start by knowing our own interior. You see, to listen openly without fixing, judging, hurting inadvertently or otherwise inflicting additional harm, we need to know where that rogue and blindsiding emotion is going to bubble up. We have to know our own triggers. We have to know the words, actions, body language, or co-opted language that is going to spark a reaction in ourselves. For instance, I don't like that people co-opt John

---

12 Heath and Duggins, *Missional. Monastic. Mainline.,* 29.

Wesley to prove a specific point that I believe is not consistent with his overall teachings. I don't like that people co-opt Jesus as if Jesus chose anything over love. I don't like proof-texting. These things trigger me. I have an immediate reaction that I have to immediately intercept if I am to listen well. I don't always do that smoothly. Chances are none of you reading this do it perfectly. In a lot of difficult conversations or disagreements, almost inevitably, I have my own opinion. That's okay. Don't let it stop you. But be aware of it. Put it aside as best you can in the moment and unpack it later.

Cooperate with God. We do it with open ears, eyes, hearts, and minds. We hold the conversation. By hold I mean that we let it go on where it needs to go unless it goes to a place that is harmful. In a group, we have to intercede if words become harmful or hurtful. Ironically, during holy listening, some voices may need to be briefly intercepted. Harmful and hurtful words do not have a welcome place to land. "I believe" is okay. "You should or you should not" usually is not okay. "Those people" is generally not a helpful description. Remember that to others, we might be "those people." We have no right to tell others what they can or should feel, think, or believe. We do have the right to let them express how they feel, think, or believe and to receive it. We do not have to agree with it. We are not expected to fix it, correct it, affirm it, or critique it. That is God's place and is between that person and God. We must always, always, always remember that each person is on his or her own journey. Our role is to be a good companion—not to decide the path for that person or group. Remember, whoever is speaking is a beloved child of God. Resist the urge to change the thinking or feeling and let it be expressed. Receive it and honor it and cry later if you need to.

Releasing the outcome perhaps takes the most trust in the listening process. If you are being present and attentive to both those you are listening to and to the nudges of the Holy Spirit, then you also must trust that the best you can do is the best you can do. Additionally, in the course of discussion, you may be asked for your own opinion. I believe that the dynamics of the group or person you are talking to make that a contextual decision. Some groups will just assume that you believe as they believe. Or they may not. If you decide to weigh in with your own opinion if asked, certainly do it in a respectful manner. It may or may not influence how or what the group thinks. Many people will be listening for someone to tell them what to think. Do your best to encourage them to come to their own conclusion. There is wrestling that needs to be done. Studying, reading, and prayer should be encouraged. See the resource guide in the back of this book.

In Community and Growth,[13] Jean Vanier says:

> We have to remind ourselves constantly that we
> are not saviours.We are simply a tiny sign, among
> thousands of other, that love is possible...

The rest is up to God.

---

13 Vanier, *Community and Growth,* 312.

Discussion questions:

- What are your thoughts on the concepts of holy listening, and is this something you feel equipped to do?
- How do you react when presented with an opinion you do not personally agree with? Do you quickly react? Do you ask more questions? Do you shut down?
- Do you feel comfortable sitting down with people who think, look, or behave differently than you? What makes you answer that way?

When Things FAIL:
What Coaching Teaches Us About Conflict

BY: BRET WELLS

> *"Check your emotions at the door."*

WE'VE PROBABLY ALL HEARD this admonition at one point or another. It means we desire to make clear-headed, rational decisions; it means that we do not want to be reactive or held hostage by fear-mongering, guilt-trips, personal vendettas, or nostalgia. It means we want people to resist getting defensive or taking things personally. It means we want decision-making based on the merits of an idea, not how we feel about the person who suggested it.

This statement is founded on a core belief that emotions are unpredictable, irrational, fleeting, and, typically, unreliable for decision-making.

There are only a few minor problems with this tidbit of practical wisdom: it is built on faulty assumptions. It is impractical, given that it is nearly impossible to remove emotions from the equation or separate them from our thinking. And finally, "checking our emotions at the door," to the degree that is possible, actually inhibits effective decision-making.

In truth, emotions are highly logical . . . they just operate on a logic driven by our perceptions, perspectives, experiences, and beliefs. (Which, in the end is what drives all logic.) Emotions are data: they are a function of both intrapersonal and interpersonal communication. Given the sheer amount of input we are exposed to at any given moment, our sanity and survival depend on our conscious mind's ability to compartmentalize, prioritize, focus, and create various shortcuts and mental models. Emotions can serve as a way to bring attention to stimuli that may or may not have registered in our awareness.

Yes, powerful emotions can and will shut down our capacity for higher-order thinking . . . even when we are actively ignoring or attempting to suppress those emotions. And this handy trick may well save our lives if we are faced with an unexpected immediate threat.

If a wild animal comes bounding out of cover toward us, we do not want to pause and consider the existential right of the animal to hunt or brainstorm a list of possible ways to develop lines of communication with the animal kingdom. The good news in the wild animal scenario is that as soon as our senses detect the presence of a dangerous predator, our brain releases adrenaline and cortisol, and most higher order thinking (and non-immediately-essential processes like digestion) shuts down in favor of the often maligned, "fight, flight, or freeze" response. That said, this same threat detection area of our brain is not very good at recognizing the difference between an approaching lion and a passive-aggressive comment that seems to be questioning our intelligence.

On the other hand, one of the side effects experienced by people who have experienced a traumatic brain injury to the portion of their brain that controls emotions is a diminished ability to make even simple decisions. Why? Because our thoughts and our emotions are inextricably linked. Decision-making involves value judgements . . . and value judgements rely on emotion.

As we develop greater awareness of our emotional reactions, we discover a valuable source of data. Even when this data is not directly related to the practical merits of an idea, it can help us identify sources of influence or resistance in ourselves and/or others. Without attention and awareness, emotions are still present and still influencing, but they function more like the strings of a puppet-master. Instead of having emotions, our emotions have us.

Emotions do more than influence our own thoughts and actions. They also play an important role in community and communication between individuals.

As social creatures, our emotions serve the purpose of signaling others in our "pack" about risks and opportunities. Emotions form a nearly-instant communication channel. We read emotions from others, for example by watching faces or hearing tone of voice, and then we use that data.

We don't have to be aware this is happening. It's an automatic process.

There are a variety of factors that make someone more powerful as an "emotional transmitter." Those with high status and positional authority seem to have a greater emotional influence, as do people with whom we have stronger ties.

So, in addition to affecting our own thoughts and actions, our emotions are affecting the people around us. Especially those that most look up to us and care about us.

Just as emotions serve as a feedback loop inside us, they form a feedback loop between us.

We are wired to connect.

One of the most important first steps toward effectively engaging difficult conversations with others is to cultivate deeper awareness of our own emotions and our patterns of behavior associated with those emotions.

However, as Facebook "slacktivism" has shown us, awareness alone is insufficient. Awareness doesn't create positive change or effective communication, however it is an essential starting point that allows for the possibility of both.

Cultivating awareness of our thoughts, feelings, and behaviors (and how each influence and are influenced by the others) prepares us for intentional engagement. It is vital that we develop skills in navigating our emotions; going beyond identifying what we feel to discern why we feel that way, what that feeling is trying to communicate, what else we are simultaneously feeling, and ultimately how we will choose to respond.

Awareness also allows us to more effectively practice optimism. I don't mean manufacturing a cheery disposition and declaring, "everything will be fine!" Optimism is about belief in our own agency. It is the conviction that our decisions can have an impact, that we can find a solution. Practicing optimism keeps us open to possibility. On the other hand, falling into pessimism, despair, and a victim mindset will almost guarantee that even if a solution presents itself, we simply will not be able to recognize it, or, if we do, we'll find that we lack the courage or conviction to pursue it.

And, yes, emotions are contagious. How we show up changes things. If we are going to have any hope of navigating difficult situations and conversations with others, we need to show up expecting that a way forward does exist, and that we can find it together. If we don't believe it to be so . . . well, why bother?

This is closely related to one of the fundamental questions that must be confronted by those who hope to be an effective coach. Coaching is a non-directive process that inspires, supports, and challenges people toward greater effectiveness in their personal or professional endeavors. One of the most significant benefits of coaching is that it is completely focused on helping the client refine what they truly want to accomplish and move forward based on their individual strengths, passions, and convictions. Coaches rarely give advice because a core conviction of coaching is that no one is better equipped to understand what is needed in a context than the person who is already in that context (ie. the person we're coaching).

In other words, to be an effective (and ethical) coach, we must truly believe in people. And there isn't really a way around this one: either we believe in people, find a way to develop that belief in people, or . . . well, why bother?

Like optimism in general, the coach's belief in people doesn't depend on a naïve outlook, a plastered-on smile, or a refusal to acknowledge the existence of very real challenges. But, like optimism, it does operate from the conviction that a solution can be found.

Often, our optimism (and productive conversation) breaks down because of FAILs: False narratives, Assumptions, Interpretations, and Limiting beliefs. These inner blocks are effective because they tend to sneak into our thinking without us ever noticing. However, if we are intentional about cultivating self and other-awareness, we can become more attuned to the presence of

FAILs, which allows us to address and overcome their influence. Here is a brief description of each and some tips, drawn from a coaching approach, for dealing with them.

FAILs

False Narratives—The inner critic, "gremlin," or stories we tell ourselves that in one way or another communicate that we're not good enough (smart enough, talented enough, supported enough, etc.) These are typically most evident in our deepest insecurities, but are also present in many of our more mundane experiences as well.

How to respond when you recognize the presence of false narratives:

- Draw them out into the open. Name the narrator if necessary. This can help you, or your conversation partner, recognize that the narrative, though part of you/them, is not your/their whole identity.
- Explore why that narrative is false. (Our minds are used to look for evidence to prove the false narrative, try giving it a chance to find evidence to the contrary.) Create an if/then response to replace false narrative with truth narrative. "If I hear the narrative saying X, I will remind myself that Y."

Assumptions—An expectation that because something has happened in the past, it will happen again. Assumptions operate as though the conclusion is already determined before there is sufficient data.

<u>How to challenge assumptions:</u>

- Begin by recognizing assumptions for what they are, question them, and either set them aside or consciously choose to let them go in order to take positive action.
- Primary question, "Just because that happened in the past, why must it happen again?"
- What makes it more or less likely to happen the same way?
  It is important to ask about both more and less. Asking one or the other can limit thinking to that one direction.
- What would make it more or less likely to happen a different way?
- What can we/you control in this scenario?
- What can we/you release in this scenario?

Interpretations—An opinion or judgement we create about an event, situation, person, or experience that we believe to be true. In some ways, this is the opposite of an assumption. Rather than deciding we know how something will turn out before it happens, interpretations claim to know the "why" behind something that has already happened. Interpretations ascribe motive and meaning.

<u>How to challenge interpretations:</u>

- Recognizing that there are other ways to look at something (and exploring/identifying what those might be) can lessen the power of an interpretation.
- We can begin by simply asking, "What is another way to look at that?"

- What would someone else (friend, spouse, etc.) say about that?
- What would someone with the completely opposite point of view say about the situation?
- What might have led me to say or do the same thing? *This question is particularly powerful because we often fall into the trap of assuming the worst about others' intentions, while expecting others to give us the benefit of the doubt regarding our own. This question allows us to flip the script: what are the less sinister explanations that we would hope others would recognize if we were the ones that had said or done this thing?*

Limiting Beliefs—Something you accept about life, yourself, your world, or other people that limits you in some way. Common limiting beliefs are statements that come from the anonymous they ("Everybody knows..."), or when something is stated with little or no evidence to support it; it's just an accepted fact. Stereotypes are some of the most obvious examples of limiting beliefs. The more insidious forms are often tied to cultural expectations ("this is how we do things around here,") and the self-fulfilling prophecies of labels ("I am an ENFP, so . . . ").

<u>How to challenge limiting beliefs:</u>

- How true is that, really?
- Why is that true?
  NOTE: "Why" questions can be risky. Since "why" points to motive, it is often perceived as confrontational and can cause defensiveness. However, in a situation where someone is weighed down by limiting beliefs—

especially if this creates a sense of powerlessness or a victim response—the confrontational nature can help someone move from passive victim to active agent. In the context of a difficult or emotionally-charged conversation, "how" is often a better option.

- Where does that idea come from?
- How has this belief affected you?
- What would be different if you were able to let that belief go?
- How can you let go of that belief?
- How can you put that into action, immediately?

If we hope to engage in healthy, productive conversation around difficult topics, it is essential that we begin by looking inside. What are we feeling? What do we want, hope, fear, or anticipate? From there we can look for shared meaning and shared purpose with our conversation partners. We can, through imagination or through listening, put ourselves in their position and consider what we might be feeling if we were sitting where they sit. If we can maintain this posture of curiosity, rather than giving way to FAILs, we can explore what is said and experienced with a belief that a way forward is possible. We can ask questions that are intended to elicit insight and create possibility, rather than manipulate or coerce toward our predetermined outcomes.

We can find a way forward together. It is rarely easy, but it is possible. If we don't believe that, then . . . well, why bother?

Discussion questions:

- How have FAILs trapped you in one way of thinking?
- Have you paused to ask what you are feeling? What you bring to a conversation?
- Why have you decided "to bother?"

2

Creating Space

BY: STEPHANIE EVELYN MCKELLAR

decision at a weary crossroads

HOW ARE YOU FEELING? Are you feeling exasperated from conflict; heartbroken as you take in the pieces of the home you once knew and community you once felt? Are you feeling fear or anxiety as you wonder what lies ahead? Are you feeling weary and confused, at a loss for how to move forward?

Have a seat, weary one. Sit here for a moment, and rest. No need to know how to take another step forward just yet. Let us name where we are, and breathe together for a moment.

Where covenant and connection once stood firm, now lies the possibility of departure and division. What can be fixed, healed, or restored here? Is hope too heavy to bear?

Your grief and exhaustion are real and valid. Explanation or attempts at conversation may feel pointless and fruitless; your throat may feel hoarse from trying to get a point across.

You want to find a way to repair what is broken, but you are at a loss—too tired and hopeless for creativity. Perhaps you wonder if it would be better to cut your losses and start dividing the assets.

But is that really what you want?

It may be appealing, especially at such a weary, brokenhearted space.

And yet,

Maybe, in the stillness, your heart yearns for a repair, a miracle, an alternative. Perhaps your preference would be to find a way through this messiness, together. Perhaps it is only a whisper, a fading and flickering light of hope.

It is enough.

Sit with that light, that hope, that small and meek desire for a moment. Let it breathe, let it echo in the space in your heart. Do not try to rationalize it, explain it, send it away, or even hold it. Just breathe with it.

Breathe in.

Breathe out.

For a moment, just witness it.

What was it that originally brought you here to this place and this table at the beginning? Why here? What joy, what hope, what appreciation did you once feel in this place? What new life did you discover here among this community? Can you remember and sit with how you initially felt?

Yes, but... (you might say)

There is no way.

Perhaps.

Perhaps there is a way.

What you have remembered just now, what you once felt, is not forever lost. We are co-creators of what happens at our tables. This is an invitation to awareness and ownership of that co-creating reality, that power, and that possibility. There is still hope here at this table. There is still nourishment. There is still life to be had. These bones aren't dry yet.

Let us cling to such hope together as we grieve and embrace our heartbreak. Let us cling to the hands of each other as we navigate what lies ahead. Let us create containers of safety and containers of bravery; let us re-imagine what our tables and relationships need to look like moving forward.

We can do this.

We are the people who follow the God who nurtures resurrection from death and breathes life into the driest of bones. We dwell in the Spirit who hovers over waters of chaos and speaks order and life into existence. As image-bearers of the divine, we bear abundant creative capacity. What can be hopeless when we show up to the co-creation process?

We are the people who follow Jesus, the one who would rather invite back into community and connectedness the woman caught in the vicious act of adultery than lose her life to the rightness of rules. We are the people who follow Jesus, the one who takes dirt and saliva to restore our sight and our societal ties rather than be bound by the blueprint of doctrine on Sabbath. We are led by our God into a kingdom of love, healing, and wholeness, built on unity, community, and collaboration.

We, the people called Methodists, have chosen to be united by our polity and practices rather than our doctrine. The very etymology of the name, Methodist, means we are about the *methods* of our practice, the disciplines that lead us into deeper faith and onward to perfection. We are not, at our core, people who believe the same thing all the time. We are people who strive to practice together, to encourage one another in beginning-ness, encourage one another towards perfection, embrace a theological playground that is wide in space and deep in faith that the Spirit moves among us in these practices and polity. In our infant baptism and open table we nurture a space in which to approach faith with intentionality, thought, reflection, exploration, discernment, a space where growth is nurtured and personal commitment cultivated. In the space of Methodism, one does not need to have it figured out or all doctrines addressed and adhered to before belonging at this table.

We have charted unfamiliar territory before in our personal and our communal lives. We have immense internal strength to stir up love, use the tools of grace, and nurture our compassion, listening ability, and empathy. We initially chose this space in which to dwell and contribute, this community or relationship in which to grow, and we continue to be co-creators of this space, making it safe for each other and brave for the work that lies ahead. May we acknowledge that we are all doing the best we can. Yes, even them. Yes, even you.

becoming navigators

It is okay if you do not know where to begin. Most of us do not. The ego is the one who towers in with great confidence and authority, afraid of losing any face or admitting uncertainty. Community is built around gathering in humility and co-creation, bringing together our various puzzle pieces; we navigate our way forward together. Let us become navigators of our wilderness. It is a daily step into vulnerability and the unknown, as the Israelites walked by fire and cloud, guided along by God's unshakeable presence. We are offered an invitation into presence with ourselves, our neighbors, and our Creator, and to release what lies ahead. Be here, be here now. Let us break bread and figure this out together. Let us release the fear-based narrative that says "this is not meant to be." Let us co-create this journey together, trusting that while it may be treacherous, it is courageous and important work, and we walk with the presence of our Creator. May we greet ourselves and each other as we are and determine **together** what the next step shall be.

embracing the fruit of conflict

In truth, conflict and disagreement are not necessarily the sign of things gone wrong; conflict handled well can breed intimacy, wisdom, and growth. As Jacob wrestled with God until the sparring ended with a new name and a limp, the conflict between them bred an intimacy that birthed the people of Israel and an everlasting covenant.

John Gottman, relationship therapist and researcher of the factors that lead to divorce and healthy marriages, talks about solvable and unsolvable problems in relationships. The unsolvable problems do not necessarily lead towards divorce, in fact, over 60 percent of issues in marriages are unsolvable![14] It is rather the *practices of engagement* that lead to divorce, whether or not vicious tactics are employed when dealing with problems. With the unsolvable issues, Gottman recommends strategies for overcoming gridlock. Avoided, unsolvable issues lead to resentment. Explored, they lead to an understanding of each other's dreams, values, fears, and motivations. Conflict can lead to deeper dialogue, which can lead to a more intimate and stronger relationship. Different views

14 Gottman and Silver, *The Seven Principles for Making Marriage Work*, 138.

are expected and honored with a commitment to understand the sources of disagreement and to work cooperatively towards common solutions. It frames conflict not as something to be avoided but as a natural outcome in a diverse group.

Rainer Maria Rilke's words may offer wisdom for dealing with such gridlock and these unsolvable spaces within our relational dynamics:

> Be patient toward all that is unsolved in your heart and try to love the questions themselves, like locked rooms and like books that are now written in a very foreign tongue. Do not now seek the answers, which cannot be given you because you would not be able to live them. And the point is, to live everything. Live the questions now. Perhaps you will then gradually, without noticing it, live along some distant day into the answer.[15]

We may live our way into different answers over time, but that is unlikely if we dig in our heels and define ourselves based on our differences. It is important to pay attention to what is underneath our convictions, where they came from, and how they inform and impact our sense of identity about ourselves. Cultivating safe space to better see ourselves can help with this. We often dig in our heels because there is something crucial and formational within us, something we fear losing. Can we get there to know what that "something" is within ourselves and within another?

By cultivating brave space we can better understand how we

---

15 Rilke, *Letters to a Young Poet, #4.*

each contribute to the community as a whole and the individuals therein, and work towards reconciliation. In our community and covenant, can we nurture a wide center with room for diversity? Can we distinguish the discomfort of being healthily stretched and challenged towards necessary growth from personal attack? Perhaps we can encounter God in a new way.

What convictions truly threaten us? (Whether our sense of self, our safety, our faith, our credibility and integrity.) What differences may simply confuse us or challenge something we would rather not address? Are we being personally attacked, or have we grown intolerant of difference, feeling uncomfortable, of disagreement and tension? From a space of safety, we can enter into brave space that allows us to explore these discrepancies and sift them for the deeper truth, wisdom, and ways forward.

diversity instead of division

If we opt for division, we mirror the current cultural trend: fear-based and inimical. This divisive narrative seeks to prove someone wrong, ridiculous, stupid, and out of their god-forsaken-minds to have the opinion and perspective they have. It dismisses the right to one's voice; it refuses to acknowledge another as an intentional and credible individual, motivated both by love and fear, just as we are. It refuses to acknowledge another as one who cares deeply about themselves, their families and communities, their convictions and faith, their safety, health and well-being, just as we do. This narrative dehumanizes, for it is easier to dismiss someone if we first deny them the humanity we share.

Division and dismissiveness foments our modern day wars; they helped ignite the current Syrian war: "The first demonstrations attracted hundreds of thousands of people of different faiths. So the regime stoked sectarian tensions to divide the opposition."[16] Division and divisiveness have long been the faithful companions of the oppressor. Throughout history, the powerful have employed a "divide and rule" strategy, attempted to break up concentrations of power and nurture discord among each other—a helpful tactic in the art of war if your opposition outnumbers you. Divide them, scatter them, nurture their dislike of each other, and they will do the work of destruction themselves; thus they will be easier to conquer. It is clever and brutal, aiming for the heart of personhood and unity. Employing division helps crumbling happen from within; unity is the stronger existence.

As the church we are called, invited, and equipped to model a different way: a way that breaks bread together in mutuality when the rest of the culture sets up hierarchy and divides,[17] a way that includes rather than excludes and divides. The kingdom of God is a mustard seed that dies to make shelter and provision for others, an invitation to the outcast, troublemakers, and unclean of society to come back again and again to the table and the community. Let our methods not divide, but let them heal division. For no matter how much we disagree, creating a table based on mutual personhood (rather than collective agreement) builds an intentional and strong community.

---

16 "How a victorious Bashar al-Assad is changing Syria," *The Economist*, June 28, 2018.

17 1 Corinthians 11:17-34

the process becomes our DNA

Division breeds more division. The practice of moving away over time leads to extremism. Sitting in the discomfort of diversity is crucial to our ongoing health as individuals and organizations. Otherwise, the ability to engage in conversation atrophies from a lack of exposure to disagreement and dialogue with a contrasting perspective.

Diversity benefits us. In our spiritual ancestry, Jewish leaders Hillel and Shammai modeled a practice of discussing and disagreeing, even documenting their disagreements without neatly tying them up.[18] They sat with the space to let theology be wrestled with; they did not seek to tie up all loose ends in a clean bow. In fact, "one could reasonably argue that not only Jewish law, but the very survival of the community depended on their disagreements."[19]

Community and covenant are spaces where we can allow safety and bravery to grow. In relationships, dedication to the growth process is what leads to connection, trust, and deep satisfaction. It is the process that makes us holy, not necessarily the content or side upon which we land. If we disconnect based on conceptions of holiness, we stand with the Pharisees as they scoff at Jesus healing on the Sabbath. Does our process divide, deride, and destroy? If so, we will not be able to build life with such hands. Only from a foundation of belonging, committed to connection, can we understand each other, hold each other's stories and perspectives, and get to know another's experience of God. Only from a foundation

18 Gibbs, "Disagree, for God's Sake! Jewish Philosophy, Truth and the Future of Dialogue," 2011.

19 Gibbs, 2011.

of belonging in commitment to connection can we proceed to a dialogue in bravery and growth. The process is important. If our means of protecting that which we consider important ends up tearing apart and destroying, what we have in fact preserved is division and destruction. We have not so much built up as we have torn apart. We cannot bully or shame each other into a different way of thinking, but it is possible to love each other into a new way of being.

listen to understand, not convince

Often we enter conversation with a singular focus: to convince or be convinced. From this aim, we sit in quietness without listening, we hear someone speaking while internally formulating our reply. Conversation is thus deemed successful if we bestow advice or convince them of our wisdom.

When engaging in a conversation with the intention to convince, what needed to find expression can feel stifled and blocked. Have you ever tried to share something in conversation, only to have someone interject their story, their perspective, their advice, or their agenda? Such a reply shuts down exploration and engagement.

What if instead we listened with the intention to understand? What if we sought to deeply see and know someone else's perspective and their experience? What if we realized we have the capacity, through conversation and dialogue, to listen someone into deeper existence? What if we need to be witnessed in community in order to fully know and understand ourselves? Mary Rose O'Reilly says "one can, I think, listen someone into existence, [and] encourage a stronger self to emerge."

Division and social hierarchy have built up too much voicelessness and silencing across our culture; practicing listening to understand helps us hold spaces where we discover tension and dissent. "As we listen with new ears, we not only learn to hold the tension of opposites, we also learn that doing so can open us, individually and collectively, to a new and better way of resolving the issue at hand."[20] It can be very difficult to listen in the midst of the tension of disagreement; perspectives can seem diametrically opposed. How do we remain in that kind of awkward and tense space?

For one thing, sitting in tension does not always need to have an immediate resolution. In tension, anxiety, and fear, our brains can become overloaded and flooded, and revert us to our oldest and nonverbal reptile brain. The prefrontal cortex (the thinking, reasoning, language part of our brain) goes offline, and suddenly we are reactive, panicked, and only able to hear signs of danger.

If the point of conversation is not to agree or convince, but to understand, then we can begin to create space to hear all the voices and opinions at the table. We can disagree, be flabbergasted by the opinion of another, and, still, there is room at the table for such diversity. Our conversations can find a new aim: to treat each other with the dignity and respect of having his or her own voice. One of my improv comedy teachers once told me, "Listening is the utmost sign of respect. If I interrupt someone, if I immediately

20 Palmer, "The Broken-Open Heart: Living With Faith and Hope in the Tragic Gap," 10.

respond with my thought instead of hearing them fully, I'm basically telling them, 'I'm better than you.'"

We are creatures of community who are called to shepherd each other towards our stronger selves. Blind spots and misperception run amok in our lives; we need people to see us, to hear us, and who are willing to give us safe space to work out our stories, motivations, and underlying fears and feelings, in order that we might grow into self-aware, confident, compassionate, healthy, interdependent human beings. We need first the spaces of safety in order to enter into the spaces of bravery that allow interpersonal and systemic change and reconciliation to occur.

But how? How do we enter into and engage these spaces? How do we hold what we so deeply believe, but also create space for another to believe something entirely different? How could we possible sit at the same table with someone who believes *that*, or who does not share my convictions, perspective, and opinions?

We can sit at the same table and continue to do work together. We can indeed find an alternative to division. We can remain united in diversity, in harmony without needing uniformity.

Yes. We can.

safe and brave space

How do we create this space?

How do we cultivate space for a person to encounter themselves, to grow and heal, to see and share their soul, and listen to the perspectives and souls of others so that a community can grow and heal?

How do we cultivate space where difficult issues can be addressed and deeply understood, where diversity can thrive and honor all types of humanity? How do we cultivate space where we can heal division and build bridges?

As ministers, educators, chaplains, leaders, cultivators, animators, writers, parents, humans, citizens, what is our role and process for creating space? In creating an environment and conversation where healing and growth can happen, where parties can learn to see different perspectives, and where we can pursue civil conflict that leads to greater insight, deeper community, and systems that prioritize justice and the wellbeing of all?

I researched many disciplines and demographics, inviting their wisdom to weigh in on the cultivation and facilitation of safe and brave space: *Where is it working? Where is it needed? What methods are used to establish and nurture it? When successful, what does it accomplish? How could these tools mend global injustice issues and divides so prevalent today?*

My research took me to the areas of: marital therapy, family dynamics, parenting, Parker Palmer's Circles of Trust, local church, Missional Wisdom Foundation's community hubs, co-working spaces, Godly Play, hospital chaplaincy, counseling, spiritual direction, coaching, coffee shop ministry, intentional christian community, low-income neighborhoods, community organizing, gardening, community development, nonprofit management, classrooms and universities, contexts of privilege, trauma therapy, conversation models,[21] leadership development, and improvisational comedy.

what I discovered

Not all space is created the same.

Some space needs to be "safer" than others—a place where freedom from the responses of others allows someone to listen to what is internal, to process out loud, and to let healing emerge. Some spaces need to be "brave"—they inherently involve risk, do not promise comfort, because they are about reconciliation and justice, and this type of work is not without struggle. In this case, "the language of safety contributes to the replication of dominance and subordination, rather than a dismantling thereof."[22]

Determining the needs of your space informs what type of space gets created.

For safe space, we need "an environment in which everyone feels comfortable expressing themselves and participating fully,

---

21 See the Resource pages at the back of this book.

22 Landreman. *The Art of Effective Facilitation*, 140.

without fear of attack, ridicule, or denial of experience."[23]

> It must be *real*, felt by the person in body.
>
> [For] any growth to happen, safety is a prerequisite. There is even a term called "quantum growth" that can happen when a person experiences safety internally for the first time around responsibility and choice. There is no grounding, no containment, no growth happening in an "unsafe" environment. Only survival happens.[24]

Safe space is a container that helps calm our fear responses (emotional, biological, and physiological), a container wherein we are able to bring our fully functioning brains back online, so we may think, reason, and respond to full capacity. We need safe space to heal internally, to learn what we think and feel, and to be able to process our world without the fear of punishment, abandonment, retribution, or injury. Safe space allows freedom from the responses of others or opposition. It allows realization to take place, it helps us to understand why we do something: *What is really going on within me? What is my fear? Why am I feeling so much resistance or combative energy? What is my body telling me? What is really at stake for me? Why don't I feel safe? What do I need in order to feel safe?*

The ground rules and expectations are crucial to establishing the space.

---

23 Landreman, *The Art of Effective Facilitation*, 138.

24 Jennifer Christian, professional counselor, conversation, April 17, 2018.

safe space guidelines:

- Embrace silence, let it speak as another party.
- A third thing (poem, story, podcast, etc) can be a helpful tool for facilitating vulnerability without feeling too exposed; they can work through the internal without having to own how personal it is.
- Release the outcome and move forward with open questions and a sense of wonder. Cultivate a space of exploration.
- Listen to understand. Listening the soul into existence, selfhood, and inner wholeness. (Instead of listening to respond, fix, or dismiss someone's experience.)
- The point is not to be right, but to nurture the expression from each person, and to honor everyone's inner teacher and wisdom.
- Inner work must be invitational.
- Honor confidentiality.
- Nurture a sense of belonging without having to first perform, sign up, believe, or agree.
- Literally facing each other, in a circle or around a table, allows everyone to see each other, to cultivate empathy, and to build mutuality.
- Safety is felt in the body, it is not convinced. This is especially true if someone has been in a survival mode. The individual gets to claim this experience of safety, not the facilitator.
- Know each other. Like each other. Respect each other.

Brave space, on the other hand, is a container applied to relationships and systems that need mending. We need to create brave

space in order to heal divides, eliminate oppression, and disman-
tle systemic injustice. Brave space involves a willingness to risk,
a move into conflict with courage and civility, and a willingness
to learn how we have been culpable or benefitted from a system
that has injured or denied others. We need brave space to speak
our truth and to listen to the truth from others. In brave space,
participants are willing to sit in feelings of vulnerability and fear.
Brave space inherently involves risk, it does not promise comfort.
This space is about reconciliation and justice, and these cannot
be achieved without being willing to face real impact (despite
good intentions), effect (despite ignorance), and systems of privilege (despite well-meaning individuals). This work is not without
struggle, sacrifice, repentance, and deep listening.

For brave space, we need "courage rather than the illusion of safety,"[25] for "we cannot foster critical dialogue regarding social justice
if we are not willing to be vulnerable and exposed, and to encounter perspectives that are shocking and painful."[26] A facilitator is
especially important for establishing and moderating the space.

brave space ground rules, enhanced:

You may have heard it said: "agree to disagree."

But, this can lead to a retreat from conflict; some may disconnect
to avoid discomfort. This practice over time can lead to an extremism in one's views, for the ability to dialogue has atrophied from a
lack of exposure to disagreement and dialogue.

---

25 Landreman, *The Art of Effective Facilitation*, 141.

26 Landreman, *The Art of Effective Facilitation*, 141.

Some of the richest learning springs from ongoing explorations of conflict, whereby participants seek to understand an opposing viewpoint. Such exploration may or may not lead to a change or convergence of opinions, or one side winning the debate, but neither is these among our objectives for our students; we find these outcomes to be reflective of a patriarchal approach to conflict, in which domination and winning over others to one's own point of view is the goal.[27]

Instead, aim for **controversy with civility.**

This allows for different views to be anticipated and honored with a group commitment to understand the sources of disagreement and to work cooperatively towards common solutions. It frames conflict not as something to be avoided but as a natural outcome in a diverse group. This can apply to communities, racial or other tensions, even interpersonal relationships.

You may have heard it said: don't take things too personally.

However, "the view that we can and should demonstrate such control is reflective of patriarchy, whereby emotional restraint—a normally masculine behavior—is unjustly overvalued."[28]

Instead, **own your intentions and impact.** Good intentions

---

27 Landreman, *The Art of Effective Facilitation*, 143.

28 Landreman, *The Art of Effective Facilitation*, 145.

matter, but there may be a better way to behave that has a better impact on the rest of the community.

You may have heard it said: challenge by choice.

Meaning: you do not have to step into challenge unless you choose to do so. But **ask yourself, what factors influence your decision about whether to challenge yourself** on a given issue? Recognize that "privilege enables them to make the choice not to challenge themselves, and that oppression often invalidates such a choice for 'target group members.'" [29]

You may have heard it said: engage with respect.

This is wonderful. However, the concept of respect may be more nuanced than clear. In what ways does someone demonstrate respect for *you*?

Instead, aim for an awareness of **multi-partiality**. The objective is not to find a consensus, but to maintain increased mindfulness of the different ways people can demonstrate respect towards one another.

Finally, *you may have heard it said: No attacks.*

This is a great ground rule, that only needs a little bit of augmentation.
Aim for: **clarifying conversation**. Describe the difference be

---

29 Landreman, *The Art of Effective Facilitation*, 147.

tween a personal attack on an individual and a challenge to an individual's idea or belief or statement that simply makes the individual feel uncomfortable.

co-creating containers of grace

We all share responsibility to help facilitate and nurture these spaces. In that role, we will celebrate the bravery of these two spaces. As peacemakers, voice-nurturers, space-protectors, threshold guides, intentional listeners, and empathetic understanders, may we be attentive to our own internal work, and practice releasing the outcome for faithfulness to the co-creation process of these spaces.

I argue that we need both spaces to work in concert with each other.

We need **safe space** to heal internally, to hear and see our voices and souls, to learn what we think and feel, and to be able process our world without fear of punishment, loss of relationship, retribution, or injury.

The objectives of safe space are:
> to stretch the muscles of using our voice to share our story and experiences;
> to make meaning, invite creativity, and cultivate authenticity;
> to engage without trying to convince;
> to listen someone into deeper existence,
> to create a container so that others may express themselves

without trying to get the right answer;

We need **brave space** to heal relationships and systemic issues. Brave space involves a willingness to risk, to move into conflict with courage and civility, and to hear how we have either been culpable, or benefitted from a system, that has injured others. We need brave space to speak our truth so others can hear from us.

> The objectives of brave space are:
> to stretch our capacity to listen to those with whom we disagree;
> to engage with wonder and curiosity;
> to understand each other's perspectives;
> to stretch our comfort level with sitting with different perspectives;
> to bring all voices to the table to explore what reconciliation and community look like that honors all humanity and creation;
> to heal relationships, rifts, and to re-humanize each other and the other.

As global and local citizens, we can cultivate spaces of dialogue in the hopes of alleviating a sectarian divisiveness that sweeps through our cultural narratives.

As humans, we can create these spaces that help bridge divides, transforming our community and homes.
As Christians and people of faith, we can lead with the confidence that grace abounds, and we can create space in our faith

communities to sit and be knit together at the table.

As leaders and the church, we can facilitate spaces where people can first know their own internal safety and wisdom, and then enter with that wisdom and humility into brave spaces.

knit us together

We can do this.

You have picked up this book because you seek, or have within you, a glimmer of hope. It is in you picking up this book, and in those that contributed to writing it and bringing it together. It is in the heartbreak you feel and the hopefulness you yearn to restore. It is in the desire for dialogue and the willingness to remain at the table.

We can do this.

Let us gather at the table of welcome and offering, of compassion and communing, of bread and brotherhood, of friendship and family.

May the Spirit of our living, breathing, creating, sustaining, redeeming God knit us together.

3

Committing to Conflict

BY: ANDREA LINGLE

"War isn't conflict. War is the inability to handle conflict."
Peter Rollins

"Do not press me to leave you or to turn back from following
you! Where you go, I will go; where you lodge, I will lodge;
your people shall be my people, and your God my God.
Where you die, I will die—there will I be buried. May the LORD
do thus and so to me, and more as well, if even death parts me
from you!" Ruth 1:16–17

THERE ARE MOMENTS IN our lives as persons and as communities
when we face a choice to devolve into war or commit to conflict in
community, to value being right more dearly than being in relationship, or to be willing to value that which we believe over those
whom we love.

If you have ever observed a group of children (a demographic of humans who, according to Jesus, comprise the Community of God), you will know that humans engage in conflict frequently and with great vehemence. There are times that children will leap across a playing field or board, intent on destroying whatever is opposing their will. Caretakers get worn out trying to force recalcitrant children into civilized behavior.

Because conflict is deep within us.

Jacob wrestled with God; Moses insisted that God feed, water, AND accompany the whiny Israelites; Jesus flipped the tables in the temple. Humans are prone to conflict, but conflict is not war. War is, according to Peter Rollins, when you can no longer remain in conflict without wanting to kill the other. The process of engaging in civil discourse begins with committing to conflict because until all participants in the dialogue are willing to come to the table, knowing that they disagree yet committed to work hard to remain in the difficult space of conflict, disagreement will lead to war or abandonment.

When someone stands in opposition to you the temptation is to dehumanize them. To make their agenda all bad or all flawed. In psychology, this is a defense mechanism called splitting. While this strategy does defend the mind and self against trauma, splitting creates an other.

An other is someone or some group that becomes dehumanized because their experience does not reflect our own.

Human subjectivity is a philosophical and psychological construct wherein each person views the universe from the isolation of the self. A self-centered universe. My lived experience is my basis for my understanding and view of the universe.

Early in my pregnancies, I found that I had a deep sense of harboring something profoundly other than myself. As my babies grew to just beyond what I considered my inner capacity, their jabs and rolls emphasized their not-me-ness. When they were delivered into the world, they opened their eyes on the bright delirium of air and light and space and slowly began to discover their subjectivity. And it is at that moment, the moment when a child realizes that they are a self, that subjectivity begins. This could be called the beginning of our commitment to conflict. Our struggle to simultaneously maintain and destroy our self.

In these pages you are going to be asked to commit to conflict: to conflict that has, at its core, a refusal to go to war. Commitment that will require each participant to face themselves and others. It will require that each participant decide if community and relationship—a paradigm of loving neighbor and self—is worth fighting for. Yes, fighting.

If we refuse to acknowledge the fights we are already in, we will never learn to fight in a holy way. We will cling, reactively, to our own subjectivity determined to destroy that which opposes us.

In gathering around a table, we intentionally place ourselves in front of our universal dependence: our need for nutrition. No matter how different our opinions are, we all must eat. No matter how different our educations have been, we all must eat. No matter how different our understandings of God are, we all must eat. So, we gather to eat, mutually dependent, individually committed to stay at the table, corporately determined to wrestle with what it means to be the Community of God.

THE GATHERING

Words of Gathering

Gather all participants in the eating space and read these words aloud together:

God in Community,

We gather today as a sign that we are willing to engage in the work of community. We acknowledge that we have come with our selves, our pasts, and our fears. Give us the courage to inhabit this place in a holy way.

Setting the Table

Setting the table is an act of radical intention. It is making room for each participant—for their needs, experiences, and desires. Set the table as a community, being mindful of each person whose place is being laid. As each place is laid, these words of commitment may be offered:

Spirit of Grace, may [participant's name] be met with grace, held in respect, and guided toward wisdom.

When the table is set, gather the group around the table and share this blessing (the blessing can be read responsively or as a group):

Table Blessing

For the Work Among us, **we pray**

May we remain here
within our bodies
among our Body
grounded in breath
breathing in shared Spirit

May we sit and break bread

not brotherhood

among a God who calms storms

orders chaos

breathes life into dry bones

resurrects the dead

May we sit and break
bread
not covenants
among a God who bleeds
and weeps
and restores the lost and cast out

Bring us into oneness

order the chaos within and among us

May we join your creativity

and compassion

amidst conflict and struggle

keep us wrestling

mend our hearts

even as we stumble and limp

so that we might

together

be your Body

made one

in your image.

creating

redeeming

sustaining

May this space at the table knit us together.

Amen.

Breaking Bread

After the food is served, have one of the participants read the following:

By gathering around this table, we intend to listen to the stories of the other. We will not use words or gestures to harm. If conflict arises, we will remember that it is the work of this space to engage in holy conflict. We commit to holding the personhood of the other as precious.

Amen.

As you begin eating, notice any tension and awkwardness in the area. Allow it to be present. Notice how the conversation rises. Notice the passing of the food. After the meal is underway, begin the practice.

A Practice of Storytelling and Listening

BY: WENDI BERNAU

Preparation:

Listening well is a sign of respect for another person. When listening, we are willing to entertain the notion that our idea may not be the best one, the right one, or the only one. In order to truly hear another person, we set aside our personal agendas. It can be difficult to let go of internal impulses to fix, correct, or advise others, which may be accompanied by finger-pointing: "You should do or think this or that instead." Sometimes we are even unconsciously thinking competitively: "I did that, too, only better" or "I was more miserable than you were." As we encounter other people, we practice releasing worrying about how to respond and creating hospitality for the other person by listening.

For this group exercise, we will practice listening to one another tell one-minute stories and talk about the experience of telling and listening. The debrief is always the most crucial piece of any kind of practical exercise, because debrief reflection is where the learning happens. If there is no intentional focus on awareness and we cannot name our internal emotions and responses, we will be held as unchanging captives to them. We want to develop the skill of listening to understand rather than listening to reply. Our goal is to pay attention to and improve our own ability to listen well so that we honor one another.

This activity has a Part I and a Part II. Part I uses fictional stories; Part II uses true stories. Each part should have its own reflection time for debriefing and comparison. The facilitator will announce the topics, keep time, and guide the pairs through all the swapping and position-switching [Note to the facilitator: be sure to pay attention to the order of telling and listening as indicated in the instructions so that everyone has the opportunity to tell first AND to listen first in each part. This is an important comparison piece in the reflection time].

The Activity

Part I:

Choose one person to be the facilitator. Divide the remainder of the group into pairs (if possible). Each pair will have a person A and a person B. All pairs will do this activity simultaneously in their own pair, so that when person A does something, it is all of the persons A in the room doing that thing at the same time; same is true for persons B.

The facilitator will announce the topic and keep track of the time.

Topic: The Time I Rode an Elephant
Time: one minute

The first story topic is the time I rode an elephant. It does not have to be a true story. In each pair, person A will have one minute to tell while person B listens. After one minute, the stories will stop where they are. The facilitator will ask the persons to swap roles, so that persons B, using the same topic (the time I rode an elephant), have one minute to tell a story while persons A listen. When one minute is up, all stories will cease.

The facilitator will shuffle the pairs so that the person A in each group finds a new person B.

Topic: The Time I Met a Famous Person
Time: one minute

The facilitator will announce a new topic. The story topic is now the time I met a famous person. Again, it does not have to be a true story. This time persons B tell first. The persons B will have one minute to tell the story while persons A listen. The facilitator will verbally announce the end of the minute and all stories will stop wherever they are. The pair will swap roles so that persons A will tell a story on the same topic (the time I met a famous person), while persons B listen. When one minute is up, the facilitator will verbally announce the end of the minute and all stories will cease.

The facilitator will ask everyone to return to their original pair, where they told and heard the story on the first topic (riding the elephant). This time, person B will tell person A's story back to person A. This means person B will have to remember what person A had said about riding the elephant. The facilitator will verbally announce the end of the minute. The persons will swap positions so that persons A will now tell persons B's story (about riding the elephant) back to persons B.

Repeating this process, persons A will find their second partners B. In one minute, persons A will retell the story of the meeting the famous person back to persons B and after that minute is up, they will switch positions so that persons B have one minute to re-tell persons As' story back to persons A.

Bring the full group together for debrief.

Questions for Reflection, Part I:

Allow a few moments for participants to silently consider the experience, then discuss the following questions:

- How was that experience? What happened?
- Did anyone get paired with a particularly good listener?
- How did that make you feel?
- What did you notice going on inside your own head during this exercise?
- How well did you remember the other person's story? Why might that be?
- Did you find it easier to listen well if you were telling your story first or second?
  Note: it is difficult to listen well if we are preoccupied with what we will say on our turn.
- What was challenging about this experience?
- What did you learn about your ability to listen?

Part II:

The facilitator will once again announce topics and keep time. Divide the remainder of the group into pairs, preferably different pairs than in Part I. Each pair will have a person A and a person B.

Topic: The Time I Felt Overlooked
Time: one minute

The facilitator will announce the topic: a time when I felt overlooked. This should be a true story. Person B will go first, and will have one minute to tell a story about a time he or she felt overlooked while person A listens. After one minute, the facilitator will announce the end of the time and all stories will cease. Persons A and B will swap roles and now persons A have one minute to tell a story about a time he or she felt overlooked while persons B listen. The facilitator will announce the end of the one minute and all stories will cease.

Shuffle the pairs so that all persons A find new persons B. It is preferable to have a totally new partner if possible.

Topic: The Time I Felt Noticed
Time: one minute

The facilitator will announce the new topic: a time when you felt noticed. This time persons A will go first, with one minute to tell a story of a time he or she felt noticed while persons B listen. After one minute, the facilitator will announce the end of the time and all stories will cease. Persons will swap roles so that persons B will have one minute to tell a story of a time he or she felt noticed while persons A listen.

Return to the original pair (a time when you felt overlooked), and just as in Part I, persons A will tell persons B's story back to them. The facilitator will announce the end of the one minute and stories will cease. Persons A and B will then swap positions and persons B will tell persons A's story back to them. The facilitator will announce the end of the minute and stories will cease.

Pairs will reunite with the persons from the second topic: a time you felt noticed and repeat the process of retelling one another's story, swapping positions after one minute increments.

Bring the full group together for debrief.

<u>Questions for Reflection, Part II:</u>

Give the participants a few moments to silently consider the experience. The facilitator may choose to repeat some of the questions from Part I and add the following:

- What did you experience this time?
- Compare listening to the fictional stories and true stories. How was that different?
- Was it easier or more difficult to listen well to a true story? Why or why not?

  Note: it is often easier to listen to a true story because of the personal content or emotional investment of the storyteller and listener in true stories; participants may also notice internal pressure of trying to honor the other person by being accurate about the details; again—our ability to listen is often tied up in our own ego, either because of worrying about the response or preoccupation with one's own story.
- What did you learn about your own ability to listen?
- How is listening to another person a sign of respect?
- How does listening open us to willingness to change?
- Am I listening to reply or am I listening to understand?

Discussion

Use the discussion questions at the end of the selected essay to guide a discussion.

Reflection

As the meal ends, take a moment to reflect. If it is helpful, one participant can read these questions aloud:

- What about this discussion encourages me?
- What about this discussion makes me angry? Why?
- What can I learn about myself?
- What have I heard? What have I refused to hear?

Clearing the Space

After the reflection is over, all participants will work together to clear the table, wash the dishes, sweep the floor, and return the space to order. This is done to symbolize that even through conflict, we are committed to compassion, grace, and peace.

After the eating space is returned to order, gather for a closing benediction.

Words of Benediction

We scoff, We dismiss, we neglect, we hurt.
We fight and we argue, instigating strife and pain.

May we remember that we belong to the God of all creation.
May the God of peace breathe peace upon us as we seek it. And once we find it, may we hold on to it tightly—not forgetting, but wholly forgiving.

Ever present God, we devote ourselves to the covenant of Love that Your Son established on Earth—**may we serve you and love our neighbor as ourselves with the unadulterated love you bestow unto us.**

Amen.

ESSAYS

Community

BY: LARRY DUGGINS

To get right to the point, we are made to be together.

THE FIRST PART OF that observation is that "we are made." A fundamental part of our Christian witness is that God—the Creator—had a hand in bringing us into existence. Whether you, as a Christian, are one who reads the creation stories in Genesis as literal descriptions of how we came into being or one who sees the complex scientific explanations of our evolution as a reflection of God's being, Christians believe that somehow God made us. And our belief goes even further—we believe that we are made in the image of God. We see all of creation as God's handiwork, but we see humanity as special, as a reflection of God's goodness and creative energy. When all of humanity stands for a family portrait, the family resemblance to our Creator-Parent is obvious.

The second part of that observation is "made to be together." Because we are made in the image of God, we are reflections of who God is, and God is always in community through the Trinity. Father, Son, and Spirit—and including all of the other descriptions we try to use to grasp the nature of the Three Persons—are always together, yet always individuals. The Three-in-One is an archetype, an example of perfect community, and our expressions of community are most certainly less than perfect. The important observations, though, are that the desire to form community is God-given and that being together is part of the very nature of God. (For a complete discussion of this topic, please see my book *Together: Community as a Means of Grace.*)

The creation story in Genesis is punctuated by the Creator's assessments of the various aspects of creation as they came to be. The land and sea were good, the growing plants were good, the living creatures were good, and the entirety of Creation, according to Genesis 1:31, was supremely good. In fact, the first thing that God notices that is not good, in Genesis 2:18, is that the person he created was alone. Nothing other than another person could fill the void in the man's life. The need for community arose from the very beginning.

And when the humans made the choice to use their God-given free will to make a choice that was contrary to God's wishes, one of the consequences was damage to community, and the tear in community hurt. They were no longer allowed to enjoy the close connection they had to God. The change in the intimacy of the relationship with God was painful, but God did not choose to abandon them—God clothed them and left them together to help each other.

Later in the story, when Cain killed Abel in a jealous rage, part of the consequences to Cain was a separation from human community. His great fear was that he would be a perpetual wanderer and that anyone he encountered would attack him. God removed him from the community he knew, but then marked him (Genesis 4:15) so that the possibility for him to build new connections with different people existed. Even in a response to a horrible crime, God knew that Cain needed community. In these and other ways, the very first books of the Bible teach us about the importance of being together.

Unity is also a recurring theme in the New Testament.

Being together as one is the theme of Jesus's beautiful prayer on the night of his betrayal (John 17), and I address that prayer in chapter 6. For now, let's hold the idea that Jesus prayed that we might be one, with him and with each other, as Jesus is one with the Father. Jesus prays that we will be drawn together so closely that we also enter into the archetype of community.

The apostle Paul spent a huge amount of his time and energy helping groups of people figure out how to be communities and how to resolve disagreements within communities. In 1 Corinthians his letter addresses a new church that is working through how to deal with old traditions, new revelations, and uncertain directions in their lives together. The issues that they faced included rival factions under different leaders, racial and ethnic differences between Jews and Gentiles, the collapse of the traditional cultural norms around sexuality, and the declining relevance of the historic guidelines for living found in the Torah. Paul provided specific advice and counsel on each of these issues, and then, in 1 Corinthians 12, he steps back to address all the specific issues with a teaching about community.

Paul creates an analogy for the people, saying that the church is like the Body of Christ. His point is that each member of the community is part of an interdependent whole and we need every part to be healthy.

He begins by observing that people have different gifts and graces and all of them flow from God. Through a variety of gifts, the Holy Spirit acts in the world through different individuals, and the actions of the individuals combine to form the action of God. Every individual makes a contribution that only they can bring because of their specific gifts and experiences.

Each of the individuals in community are valuable, and all are part of the body, regardless of their origin or status. Within the body, the distinctions of Jew and Gentile, of slave and free, become irrelevant. All of the body parts are important. Further, it does not make sense for one part of the body to dismiss another. Paul almost lapses into comedy as he imagines an ear lamenting that it is not an eye or an eye saying to a hand, "I don't need you." (1 Corinthians 12:21) Each part of the body performs a unique function within the body that is necessary for the body to thrive.

He pulls this idea further forward as he observes that each body part ought to share mutual concern for the other body parts. Paul observes that pain in a single body part can bring pain to the entire body, so the parts need to care for the whole, not simply for its own needs and health. Keeping all the body parts functioning and healthy supports the life of the body. Paul goes on to expand the idea of mutual care in 1 Corinthians 13, the famous chapter on love. Patience, kindness, humility, truth, endurance—all of the characteristics of love—are needed to care for the parts of the body.

Scripture is filled with examples of God acting in and through community. Whether organizing new churches or responding to great sin, God acts to maintain and preserve community in many forms. Jesus prays for us to become one, and, recognizing that that might take a while, Paul teaches us to value each individual. Paul reminds us that we are hurt when someone else is hurt, and that we are diminished when someone else leaves. Paul calls us to work hard to hold our community together through love.

Discussion questions:

- How do you react to the idea that we are made to be in community?
- Spend a minute with Genesis 2:18–24. What does the scripture tell you about who can fill a person's need for community? How narrowly should we read this passage—does it apply to more than love between one man and one woman?
- Think about the types of conflicts Paul faced in Corinth. How are they different from the conflicts we face in society today? Does that affect your reading of the scripture?
- How does Paul invite us to handle conflict?

River of Change

BY: KATHRYN HUNTER

RECENTLY, MY HUSBAND AND I enjoyed three days of camping beside the beautiful Edisto River in South Carolina. The Edisto is the longest, free-flowing, blackwater river in North America. At first glance, the river appears to be still and calm, but, if you watch closely, you can see that it is flowing swiftly and relentlessly towards the ocean.

The story of God's relationship with humanity is much the same. It is a relentless, never-ceasing flow directed by God and towards God's perfected kingdom. This story of redemption is about God's mercy and love, always flowing towards reconciliation and healing but often with unexpected twists and bends.

In general, we, humans, do not like twists and bends. We prefer a set pattern. We want to know the plan! We want to know every detail of what is going to happen along the way. There is comfort in rules and boundaries. However, sometimes the rules change. What do we do then?

God gave rules, commandments, and codes to guide humanity's way of being in this world, but, time and time again humans failed and proved unable to live up to God's holiness and justice. The nature of God is unchangeable so God's love will not allow humanity's weaknesses to keep us from God. In God's greatest moment of love and redemption the Christ was born. God Incarnate came to live among us and to reveal God to us.

The Promised Messiah arrives but is not at all what has

been expected. Something new is happening. Christ puts love and welcome above rules and laws. For Christ, the greatest command- ment is to love. He healed on the Sabbath because healing people is more important than strict observance of the Sabbath. Christ touched lepers, ate with sinners, and befriended women. This unconditional love and disregard for some rules was not appreci- ated by the Pharisees, the rule keepers of that day. And so, on the cross, (in the most amazing twist of all!) Christ died for the world and was raised victorious over sin and death.

The river flows on in the early church. In the Book of Acts chapter 10 we find an amazing account of the Spirit moving and of age-old, sacred rules changing. In a vision, Cornelius, a devout Gentile, was told to send for Peter to come to his house. So, Corne- lius sent two slaves and a soldier to find Peter. A short time later, Peter also had a vision and was told to eat what the Jewish rules had always declared unclean. When Peter protested that he had always been a rules keeper and so could not eat, the Spirit said, "Do not call unclean what I call clean." As this vision came to an end, there was a knock on the door and there stood the three men sent by Cornelius with the invitation to come to his house.

Now for Peter, a Jew, entering the house of Cornelius, a Gentile, was completely forbidden by Old Testament law. Peter would have never done that before his vision. Peter chose obedi- ence to the Spirit over the rules and entered the house of the Gentile centurion. As Peter proclaimed the Good News of Jesus Christ, the Holy Spirit fell mightily on them all. When Peter and the other Jews who had come with him, saw that God accepted the

Gentiles and filled them with the Holy Spirit, they gladly baptized them and welcomed them as Christians.

Because we live in such a different time and place, it is hard for us to really feel the impact of this change, but this was huge for Peter and for his fellow Jewish Christians. They had always believed that their holiness and righteousness came through their obedience to the rules and to being God's chosen, separate people. Now, they see that God is welcoming all. Love is placed above rules.

Do you think that this acceptance of Gentiles was easily accepted by Peter's fellow Jewish Christians?

It was not. Peter's actions were criticized and he was called to Jerusalem to give an account to the leaders of the church. Conflict arose.

Change is rarely easily accepted. Change of our religious traditions are even harder to accept. The mere thought that our faith traditions may change is traumatizing! It is as if we have found a rock on the bottom of the river to stand on and then, suddenly, we are swept away by the flow of the water. We find ourselves struggling and flailing to find something to hold onto and what we really want is to hold onto that old rock that served us for so long!

Change is inevitable—even within the church. So, what are some possible means of coping within our faith community with the fear and conflict that may arise in times of change?

Because this fear of change is an almost universal reaction, we can feel empathy and patience towards those struggling in times of change. Listen for ways you can connect with those who may have different views from you but have the commonality of struggling with change. Such as: we fear different things but we both fear! Perhaps as community, we can acknowledge our fear and encourage one another in our common faith in the One who says, "Peace, be still."

Another helpful means of coping with change is to consider how God has brought us through such times in the past. God has carried us through in the past and will continue to do so. We have seen twists and turns in the river during our lifetimes. There was a time in the not so distant past, that many in the church thought slavery was okay, after all, the Bible condoned it. Most of us no longer believe a woman must cover her head in church, instead we believe God calls women to preach!

All of these rule changes have caused conflict. They have not come easily. In these uncertain times in the United Method-ist Church, we all desire to remain faithful to God and to scrip-ture, and we all are devoted to our Wesleyan traditions and theology. We may just see them from different perspectives. Our acknowledgement of our common desire to serve our God and our common dependency on our God's grace bind us together as the river flows on.

Closing Prayer:

Gracious Redeemer,

You are always working with love and grace in our lives and in the life of your church. May we open our hearts to the work of your Holy Spirit. Give to us the gift of trust that we may rest in you and flow in your River of Life.

We thank you for companions who travel with us, and may our love for one another give us strength and reveal your love to the world.

In Christ's name we pray,
Amen.

Discussion questions:

- What are some changes you have witnessed in the church of today and the church of yesterday?
- Have you experienced a shift or change in your own theology and thinking as you continue your faith journey?
- Consider this quote from the prayer of Pierre Teilhard de Chardin:

> Above all, trust in the slow work of God. We are quite naturally impatient in everything to reach the end without delay. We would like to skip the intermediate stages. We are impatient of being on the way to something unknown, something new. And yet, it is the law of all progress that it is made by passing through some stages of instability—and that it may take a very long time. Above all, trust in the slow work of God, our loving vine-dresser.

What speaks to you in this quote?

Catholic Spirit

BY: LARRY DUGGINS

IF WE COULD HAVE asked John Wesley to contribute an essay to this volume, I am convinced he would have given us his sermon "Catholic Spirit."[30][31] According to Albert Outler,[32] Wesley first preached this text in 1740, repeating it twice again in 1749. Outler argues that John Wesley's mother, Susanna, belonged to a strain of Anglicans who discouraged emphasis on creeds, doctrines, and restricting theologies, and she taught this approach to her son. John Wesley developed a healthy skepticism regarding rigid statements of truth, and, at the same time, held strongly to what he believed to be the core of Christianity.

Wesley's sermon was based on 2 Kings 10:15 in which Jehu, a king of Israel anointed by the prophet Elisha, encountered Jehonadab, the founder of a tribe of Kenites who were known for abstaining from wine as part of their religious practice.[33] Jehu greets Jehonadab with the question, "Is thine heart right, as my heart is with thy heart?" Jehonadab responds, "It is. If it be, give me thine hand." Wesley draws two major points from this single verse; he perceives the question of Jehu as inquiring about a common set of basic beliefs, and he perceives the response

---

30 Outler, *The Works of John Wesley Vol. 2*, 79.

31 The complete sermon is available online at http://wesley.nnu.edu/john-wesley/the-sermons-of-john-wesley-1872-edition/sermon-39-catholic-spirit/.

32 This essay refers extensively to Albert Outler, ed., *The Works of John Wesley Vol. 2* (Nashville: Abingdon Press, 1985)..

33 Orr, "Jehonadab."

of Jehonadab as an affirmation of shared common beliefs and an invitation to join together.

Wesley argues that Jehu would likely have known about the particular beliefs of Jehonadab and his group based on a reference to their abstinence found in Jeremiah 35:3–10. Wesley emphasizes that Jehu's question did not request information on particular practices, but rather inquired as to the position of his heart. Jehu sought affirmation that Jehonadab shared a strong relationship with God rather than a confirmation that all of his worship practices precisely coincided with his own. Jehonadab's response affirmed the connection between the two men, which was a shared love of God.

Having established the thrust of Jehu's question, Wesley moves into a listing of the characteristics that he believes sit at the core of Christian belief. They include a belief in the existence and perfection of God, a faith in Christ crucified and indwelling, and an attitude of being filled with the energy of God's love. He points toward a lived emphasis on the will of God, a focus on doing good, and an attitude of loving all, including neighbor and enemy. He concludes his list with an established practice of showing love in one's daily works.

Wesley then draws distinctions between the core Christian beliefs and things which fall outside of the core. He lists many things that he believes fall outside of the core that have actually caused warfare between Christian groups, including worship structures, ecclesial structures, modes of baptism, and the use of alcohol. These things, Wesley argues, should not affect the love between Christian people. He does not diminish their importance, but he believes that the importance of the connectional love between Christian people is simply more important.

Christian love, Wesley explains, should include a general desire for the well-being of each other. It should include prayer for each other and encouragement of each other, including supporting one another through difficulties and "provoking" each other to do good works. Mutual love should be supported by actions, not simply words.

Wesley concludes his sermon by cautioning against indifference. He draws a strong distinction between the core beliefs, which are vital and non-negotiable, and practices which fall outside of the core. He confronts theological stances of his day that allowed practically all of the core of Christian belief to be questioned. He argues that each person must carefully consider and choose the practices which, in their opinion, most fully support the person's understanding and embrace of the core beliefs. Each person may vary in these selections, but not in their adherence to the core.

Wesley's approach pushes modern listeners to consider several issues when considering disagreement with other Christians. The first of these issues is the question of core beliefs. **Each Christian person must struggle with identifying and refining the aspects of Christian belief that are essential to being a Christian.** For Wesley, the core beliefs centered around the reality of God, Christ crucified and resurrected, and the indwelling of the Spirit demonstrated through God's activity in the world through Christian people. I have encountered some Christian people for whom the list would be much longer, and therein lies the friction that Wesley exposes. For example, I believe in the virgin birth of Jesus. Am I to reject another Christian who does not? Each Christian person may need to struggle with what is essential to their belief.

The next issue Wesley's sermon raises is the question of how to interact with Christian people who share a common belief in the core aspects of Christianity but differ on beliefs which are not at the core. Some of us are very comfortable working, ecumenically, across the many Christian denominations and traditions, and others of us look with suspicion at the Catholics across the street. Discussion and a sharing of Christian service in the world can be avenues to identifying shared core beliefs, while a lack of those things may lead to misunderstanding and the creation of isolated groups.

This is not to say that every group of Christians must include a wide variety of opinions and understandings, but only that differences in understandings should not lead to animosity among Christians. I enjoy the moderate consumption of alcohol and do not feel that is sinful behavior, so I might feel uncomfortable worshipping every week with a Christian group that believes in abstinence from alcohol. I can remain in connection with them through prayer, encouragement, and hospitality, and I can worship with another Christian community that welcomes my perspectives on alcohol.

This is where I feel Wesley's teaching provides a strong contrast to the public environment of conflict in modern day America. We are confronted with "news" programming in which "analysts" of differing positions argue with each other in aggressive and unpleasant ways. Politicians demean and degrade each other in a way that is infantile and embarrassing, and political and industrial forces encourage fear and factional isolation to achieve political and economic goals. In my opinion, and I believe in John Wesley's, this is un-Christian. We are called to be a people together—a single body of Christ. Division and factionalism pull us away from the unity Jesus prayed for us to share.

Discussion questions:

- If you were asked to list the Christian beliefs that are "core" beliefs for you, could you do it? Why or why not?
- Have you ever been suspicious of or uncomfortable with other forms of Christianity? What made you feel uncomfortable?
- What has been your best experience in disagreeing with someone, yet remaining connected to them? In that case, what made that possible?

Harmonious Disagreement

BY: ROBERT BISHOP

Those who eat must not despise those who abstain, and those who abstain must not pass judgement on those who eat; for God has welcomed them.

Romans 14:3

WHEN I WAS SIXTEEN years old, I was a leader in my small, rural-ish church. I spent a week over the summer at a camp that taught young people like me to lead singing in worship,[34] and I came back with some Ideas, one of which was essentially a rejection of my denomination's historical teaching on the sinful nature of the use of instrumental music in worship.[35] Our preacher caught wind of my heresy and confronted me on it, then followed up by writing a bulletin article that was a scathing review of a book he'd presumed that I'd read, then by preaching a three-part sermon series on A Capella worship as the approved Biblical pattern. He started by citing the story of Nadab and Abihu offering strange fire before the Lord in Leviticus 10, moved on to a very technical, if misinformed, breakdown of the Greek word *psallo* as found in Paul's instructions to the Ephesians to make music in their hearts, and finished up with an exhortation not to be a stumbling block, again using Pauline language (Romans 14–15 and 1 Corinthians 8–10). I suppose he figured that the matter was settled, because he never mentioned it to me again. As you might imagine, I didn't

---

34 This happened more recently than you think it did.

35 See the above footnote.

find myself approaching him much for advice on spiritual matters either. He proof-texted me in a proverbial and public slap on the wrist, and I was a kid who couldn't think of a good comeback while the bully was in the room.

Years later, as a minister in the same denomination, I watched as the smaller, somewhat less rural church in my charge argued amongst themselves over the same issues that have faced our people since its inception. (Depending on who you ask, this is either the late eighteenth century or AD 33. Either way, we've been fighting the same fights for quite some time.) I found myself preaching about stumbling blocks, but not in the same way my preacher did when I was a tenth grader sitting in the pew, everybody aware that we were suffering through this sermon series because I questioned one of our sacred cows. Instead, I zeroed in on the part of Paul's argument where he refers to the "weaker brothers and sisters" who are stumbling as a result of other Christians exercising their freedom in Christ. Are we to aspire to be weak or to be strong? Does possessing such weakness give us the right to be grumpy?

I now find myself a member of a house church, made up of people from various Christian backgrounds. Some of them consider themselves refugees of the church or perhaps of a particular denomination, while others are simply intrigued by the idea of a simple service that doesn't necessarily conform to Southern Protestant norms. We live in a town that isn't diverse by any stretch. In the last census, it was revealed that we were 90.6 percent white, which is by far the lowest that figure has ever been. The area has a history of and reputation for racism, which is well earned in my experience. Our church, like many others, is racially homogenous. In many ways, we are no more diverse than the monochromatic suburb in which we are situated.

We are different in one key way.

Our group has had families come and go over the years. In 2016, we had four core families that participated in the life of the church, and we were split exactly down the middle when it came to who we supported in the Presidential election. We've never emphasized politics, but we don't shy away from it either. Our tense arguments, full of vehement disagreement, were sometimes interrupted by the Communion meal, often presided over by a child. None of us ever convinced the others (have you ever had a conversation about politics that ended any other way?), but we never stopped showing genuine love for each other.

For unrelated reasons, we are in a liminal space right now. The future of our group is in jeopardy. One of the images that keeps me wanting to fight for the survival of this church is that of 2016, one of the most contentious years in recent memory. We weren't immune to it, and in fact we leaned into it, but we never lost sight of who we were in relation to Christ and to each other. I want to belong to a church like that.

My friend and colleague Matt Johnson observed to me recently that in the church we tend to strive for conformity rather than harmony. As somebody who grew up in an A Capella tradition, this resonates with me greatly. When we speak of harmony in the church, we aren't just referring to the eye and the hand of the body or to different roles that people play, like apostle, evangelist, and so on. There's a diversity in belief and praxis that is already present in the catholic church, and we do ourselves no favors when we parse ourselves into homogeneous groups.

We may see the food laws that were the subject of Paul's mediation as insignificant today, but these were gigantic issues for the early church as Jews and Gentiles worked out what it meant to coexist with each other. It's significant that he never encouraged them to go their separate ways. So, I choose to stay in the struggle that my faith community is experiencing because, even though it is hard, my community with worth fighting for.

I know and am persuaded in the Lord Jesus that nothing is unclean in itself . . . For the kingdom of God is not food and drink but righteousness and peace and joy in the Holy Spirit.
Romans 15:14a, 17

Discussion questions:

- What is the cost of staying in a disagreement?
- What is the cost of leaving?
- How can communities disagree without inflicting harm?

4

Encountering the Other

BY: ANDREA LINGLE

"To love another person is to see the face of God."
Victor Hugo in "Les Miserables"

Jesus, tired out by his journey, was sitting by the well. It was about noon. A Samaritan woman came to draw water, and Jesus said to her, "Give me a drink." (His disciples had gone to the city to buy food.) The Samaritan woman said to him, "How is it that you, a Jew, ask a drink of me, a woman of Samaria?"
John 4:6b–9

DUST COVERED HIS FEET, ankles, and hem. The tassels that hung from his tunic were practically furry. She hadn't seen his face. She kept her eyes on the dirt and dust, feet and ankles, hem and tassel. If she was quiet, maybe she could get her water jar filled without a scene. She could see that he was a Jew, so she should probably turn around now and wait for him to leave, but she was thirsty. So very thirsty.

The rope rolled over the support beam suspended over the hole of the well. She could feel the bucket hit the water. Now it was just a matter of a few practiced pulls and she would be away.

"Ma'am, may I have some water?"

His word made her flinch. She should have waited. She raised her eyes to his face. There was nothing there. No malice, no arrogance, no anger. Just thirst, perhaps a little tiredness, and a profound openness. A face that had asked a question. May I have some water?

Part of the work that the Missional Wisdom Foundation does is to lead spiritual pilgrimage. As a part of that work, I have had the opportunity to be part of a team tasked with working to better articulate the theology surrounding pilgrimage. Pilgrimage is a deeply mysterious process, but one of the things that I have learned is that the major difference between a spiritual retreat and pilgrimage is that spiritual retreat is a centering practice and pilgrimage is a de-centering practice, and this de-centering largely takes place when you encounter the gaze of the other. The pilgrim way, when taken in community, is profoundly de-centering, and this forces the pilgrim to acknowledge the humanity, profound belovedness, and intrinsic goodness of the other. There may be a heavy coating of irritating absurdity and gross incompatibility, but at the core of the other dwells the Divine spark of the Christ.

And that changes everything.

You must seek to truly encounter the other to engage with them in a holy way. Doctrinal differences tend to become less threatening when you are sure that the other that is beholding you, loves you. When we can see the other, not as a nameless, face-less, object, but as one called into being by love, we can allow curiosity instead of anger to direct difficult conversations.

The woman at the well, whose story is told in John 4, is initially struck, not by Jesus's miracles or power or promise. She was struck by being seen. When we see the other among us, in the full complexity of the other's difference, we are decentered and, in being decentered, are invited into a fuller understand of who God is. When we are forced to see the other as the bearer of the Divine image, we discover that God is multifaceted. No single image of the Divine gives a complete picture of the Divine.

Like the Jews and Samaritans, the differences in our holy spaces and practices can become divisive and pejorative, but, when we stop to see that even a Samaritan can supply the need of a Jew, our communities can begin to reflect a more complex, inclusive, and loving God.

THE GATHERING

Words of Gathering

Gather all participants in the eating space and read these words aloud together:

God in Community,

We gather today as a sign that we are willing to engage in the work of community. We acknowledge that we have come with our selves, our pasts, and our fears. Give us the courage to inhabit this place in a holy way.

Setting the Table

Setting the table is an act of radical intention. It is making room for each participant—for their needs, experiences, and desires. Set the table as a community, being mindful of each person whose place is being laid. As each place is laid, these words of commitment may be offered:

Spirit of Grace, may [participant's name] be met with grace, held in respect, and guided toward wisdom.

When the table is set, gather the group around the table and share this blessing (the blessing can be read responsively or as a group):

Table Blessing

For the child within you, **we pray**

For the heaviness within you
that yearns to connect

For the grief that you carry

For the ways that you've tried

We give thanks

Together,

May we find at this table

a grace that helps us

Stand

Sit

Remain

Pray

And listen

For the ways you've not
listened

For the judgments you've leapt
to

For assumptions you've made

We forgive you

May we be patient

have compassion for

ourselves

You are here

You are still trying

We are here

We are trying

We are held in the infinite

We see you and hear you

Your fear echoes ours

Our hearts seek connection

Triggered, afraid

lenses color and filter our
hearing

grace and mercy of

The God who abides

The Spirit who enlivens

The Jesus who forgives

Thank you for staying

Thank you for letting us hold
this with you

**May this space at the table
knit us together. Amen.**

Breaking Bread

After the food is served, have one of the participants read the following:

> *By gathering around this table, we intend to listen to the stories of the other. We will not use words or gestures to harm. If conflict arises, we will remember that it is the work of this space to engage in holy conflict. We commit to holding the personhood of the other as precious.*
>
> **Amen.**

As you begin eating, notice any tension and awkwardness in the area. Allow it to be present. Notice how the conversation rises. Notice the passing of the food. After the meal is underway, begin the practice.

A Practice of Mirroring

BY: WENDI BERNAU

Preparation:

People who regularly engage in community-based creative activities, such as concert bands, orchestras, theatrical ensembles, and sports teams, understand the value and importance of each individual member of the group contributing their own skill set to the larger group as they work together to accomplish a common goal. Each individual knows that he or she cannot accomplish the entire task of the group alone. Everyone must give themselves to the process of creating, to the ebb and flow of the whole as each person's part comes into prominence and subsides into the background over the course of the event. If someone insists on dominating the others in the group, the whole group suffers.

This theatrical warm-up exercise, called mirroring, offers each participant the opportunity to explore leading and following and to reflect on those experiences of stepping out and letting go. There is a time for leading and a time for making space for the other person to lead. There is also a time for finding balance and compassion as we become co-creators with one another in the third space that opens with the possibility of a new combined idea to emerge.

Mirroring is a conversation in movement without words. Participants will be leading and following one another in silence, maintaining eye contact with a partner. Prolonged eye contact can be intense for some people; participants should be permitted to disengage for a moment and re-engage as they are able.

The Activity

Form the group into two equal lines, giving room to move by standing arm's-length apart in all directions. Turn the lines to face each other and pair up with the person in the line opposite. Once everyone has paired up, the group is asked to keep silence together.

The facilitator will choose one line to begin as leaders. In each pair, the leader will move arms, legs, or head slowly and gently as the other person in the pair mirrors what the leader is doing. While pairs may begin by watching one another's arms or hands, the goal is to be keeping eye contact while following the movements using peripheral vision. This is not a time to be tricky; we want our partner to be able to follow easily.

After approximately three minutes, the facilitator will invite the lines to swap roles, so that leaders now become followers and followers become leaders. Again, the aim is to keep eye contact as partners move in sync with one another.

After approximately three minutes, the facilitator will indicate that the assigned roles are completed and pairs will continue to lead and follow one another but now no one is designated as the leader. Rather, the pair will move together with no leader and no follower—or both are leaders and both are followers—still with no talking. The only communication is the movement itself as each pair co-creates this new phase of the exercise.

After approximately three minutes, the facilitator will invite the pairs to bring their movements to a close and to choose (without speaking) one movement that will represent their time together; a movement that is their own. The facilitator should give a few seconds for the pairs to find that position and a few seconds to hold it.

Bring the group back to a circle to debrief what happened, using the following questions for discussion.

Questions for Reflection

Allow a few moments for participants to silently consider the experience, then discuss the following questions:

- What did you notice happening in your pair?
- How did it feel to be the leader/follower?
- What was your experience of having neither leader nor follower, but to co-create?
- Did anything unexpected happen?
- How did your pair choose the ending position and why was it significant for your time with that person?
- How was this experience similar or different to having a conversation with words?

Discussion

Use the discussion questions at the end of the selected essay to guide a discussion.

Reflection

As the meal ends, take a moment to reflect. If it is helpful, one participant can read these questions aloud:

- What about this discussion encourages me?
- What about this discussion makes me angry? Why?
- What can I learn about myself?
- What have I heard? What have I refused to hear?

Clearing the Space

After the reflection is over, all participants will work together to clear the table, wash the dishes, sweep the floor, and return the space to order. This is done to symbolize that even through conflict, we are committed to compassion, grace, and peace.

After the eating space is returned to order, gather for a closing benediction.

Words of Benediction

Oh God, you made us to fill in gaps—diverse and unique creations.

You gifted us with your Presence and Grace. May we be present enough with each other to never neglect those who don't fit into our preconceived notions of self and being. We are created to live in the difference, not be fearful of difference.

Ever present God, we devote ourselves to the covenant of Love that Your Son established on Earth— may we serve you and love our neighbor as ourselves with the unadulterated love you bestow unto us.

Amen.

ESSAYS

Disability, Disagreement, and Unity

BY: JUSTIN AND LISA HANCOCK

A YEAR AND A half after our wedding day, we went on our dream honeymoon to Disney World. On our first day there, we went straight to Disney Hollywood Studios, and our second ride for the day was the Rock 'n' Roller Coaster starring Aerosmith. Though Justin had never ridden roller coasters, we were excited to give it a try. Multiple people had told us about the excellent and accommodating nature of the Disney World staff when it came to helping with transfers onto rides for wheelchair users. We figured that between Lisa's transferring expertise and some help from the ride attendants, we would be fine. So, we rolled up the wheelchair accessible line of the Rock 'n' Roller Coaster ready to enjoy this first real roller coaster of our trip.

When we arrived at the front of the line, the attendant looked at us a bit strangely and informed us that, in fact, they were not allowed to help with transfers due to liability issues. For this particular roller coaster, that meant Lisa would have to lower Justin into a small roller coaster car below ground level. Transfers are not easy when moving to a small seat on the same level, much less one below the level of the wheelchair. In a move of both youthful folly and defiance, we decided we would ride the roller coaster anyway. With much awkwardness, born out of Justin's legs' propensity to not bend well, we managed the transfer and away we went.

We thoroughly enjoyed the ride, but when it stopped we

came to the crashing realization that now we had to get Justin back into the wheelchair, the seat of which was easily five feet above the roller coaster car. Lisa had still not mastered lifting Justin from the floor straight to his wheelchair, much less from below ground level. Faced with this dilemma, one might think someone would offer to step in and help. But, no. No one helped. Eventually, we determined that Justin could crawl, with Lisa's help, up, onto the platform, and then up onto the wheelchair enough that Lisa could take over, turn him around, and get him seated in the wheelchair again. Fifteen minutes later, with three ride attendants standing around watching us, we did it. We got Justin from that roller coaster car to his wheelchair—by ourselves.

There are those for whom this situation would have been the beginning of The Worst Honeymoon Ever. Whether consciously or unconsciously, those Disney employees were asking us to exist in Justin's disability from a stance of shame and extreme difference. There were certainly times during that fifteen minute crawl up the wheelchair that Justin felt like turning around and going home, and Lisa felt like a failure as a caregiver. But, as difficult as the situation was, it was the beginning of a deeply held conviction that the difference in embodiment in which our family exists is not something full of shame. Rather, it is our pride. Our existence as a disabled family is a source of strength and joy for us.

As we began our ministry within the disability community several years later, we came to our interactions with a deep sense of identity and pride in being named disabled. When people would ask Justin what he wanted to be called, he would proudly claim the label "disabled." Yet, it was not long before we came to understand that how persons identified themselves in the disability community had long been a contested issue. We encountered persons in various church congregations who viewed the label "disabled" as a source of shame and isolation. They took pride in calling themselves differently abled or identifying their children as special needs. Our initial encounters with these congregants took us aback. For us, the terms "special needs" and "differently abled" speak to nondisabled attempts to gloss over and/or sanitize the unique differences that arise out of disabled embodiments. Hence, we faced a conflict in which the moniker we claimed with pride was seen as a source of shame for others, and the moniker others claimed with pride struck us as arising from shame imposed on disabled persons by the nondisabled.

As we encountered this reality, we witnessed that many naming issues have splintered the disability community. What counts as a disability, who wants to claim disability, whether "disability" is the appropriate term, and multiple other issues can start intense arguments and debates, completely derailing productive dialogue around the disability community's efforts to advocate for themselves within the larger culture. Further, in church settings, these debates can hinder efforts to do meaningful ministry with and among the vast diversity of the disability community.

The longer we minister to persons with disabilities, the more we recognize that this conflict is but one example of what occurs when the Body of Christ spends its energy trying to win an argument without determining where the essentials lie and where there might be room to start from a place of shared connection.

Within the disability community, discussion of the Body of Christ, particularly around Paul's words in 1 Corinthians 12, takes on deep embodied meaning. Paul does not assume that the church in Corinth is going to need a running start to become the Body of Christ. Rather, Paul assumes that because they are a worshipping community, they are the Body of Christ. They, and we, do not have to earn our place in the Body of Christ, nor are some people kicked out or considered nonessential just because they might be considered less honorable (1 Corinthians 12:22–24). Further, what is even more instructive for the present-day church is Paul's stubborn insistence that persons have sacred worth simply because they are created by God. Thus, if we are all God's creations, then God values all members of the Body of Christ with the same sacred worth.

Thus, the Body of Christ is a living being in which all parts relate to the other. This interrelatedness is not foreign to persons in the disability community. One of the primary commonalities among persons with disabilities is the interdependence with which many of us live our lives. This interdependence is not merely with family members, but with the world in general. Further, in its healthiest forms, true interdependence is not demeaning, but life-giving for all involved. This is what we learned when we personally faced the deep question: how do we name ourselves disabled and still commune with others who reject this naming?

One of our first accessibility consultations was with a local United Methodist Church in the process of beginning a worship service specifically designed to be accessible for all embodiments. The senior pastor asked us to come talk to the congregation about the world of disability, disability theology, and how to have open and hospitable interactions with people with disabilities. On our drive over, we discussed how important it was to us to make sure the congregation knew that the appropriate term to use when referring to a person's disability is "disability." Before our conversation with the larger congregation began, we had a private conversation with a woman with developmental disabilities and her mother. We were having a lovely conversation when the mother declared unequivocally, "I will not use the word disabled. My daughter is differently abled." To say that we were put on the back foot is an understatement. Further, she expressed that she wanted the congregation to know using "disabled" or "disability" was not appropriate.

This conversation had a double consequence. To begin with, it was extremely humbling and instructive for us to never assume that you are in control of a dialogue before entering into conversation. To do so is folly. Second, the congregant's insistence on this point made us aware that we needed to reinforce the idea that no one person—us included—can dictate the parameters of another's self-identification or naming. Thankfully, we had a few minutes between this private meeting and the public forum to collect ourselves and adjust our approach. In the public conversation, we took the opportunity to model what accepting these different identifiers could do. We explained that naming in the disability community is contested. We explored why naming in the disability community is as diverse as one could possibly imagine, and why names are rejected by some and fully embraced by others. Finally, we boiled it down to the essentials: accept that people have different ways of claiming their embodiments, honor the way persons name themselves, and remember that the focus is not on agreeing on the names but welcoming all persons as part of the Body of Christ.

As we reflect on this incident several years later, perhaps

it is honest to admit that we would not come into the conversation with such hard and fast ideas regarding terminology and an already determined conclusion. Now, we try to present a twofold invitation to persons involved in these dialogues. First, we invite persons of all embodiments to fully rejoice in their own embodied identity and the journey that comes with it. Second, we invite these individual journeys to join with one another and do the messy, difficult work of journeying together as we grow into God's beloved, complex, and diverse community. These invitations never come separate from one another. To do one requires the other, which also means that living out our identity in the Body of Christ means honoring the sacred connection we have even as our disagreements about what to call ourselves continue. In fact, to learn to rejoice in one's disabled/differently abled/special needs embodiment may necessarily include encountering others in the Body of Christ who disagree with your naming but fully embrace your interdependent existence.

We have seen throughout our work and our growing understanding of living within a diverse community that the ability to recognize our sacred connection with another while still disagreeing about issues that are deeply important to each of us is key to the making of disciples of Jesus Christ for the transformation of the world. Engaging with and honoring the differences between us, then, becomes a critical means by which the Triune God does the work of sanctification within the unified Body of Christ. Further, by leaning on our sacred connection as members of the Body in the midst of disagreement, we are freed to continue working toward the mission of God in the world even as we grow in the midst of trying to understand one another more deeply.

Discussion questions:

- Discuss a time when you were on the edge of giving up because of a challenge you faced and how that incident inspired you to examine your own views more deeply than before.
- Have you ever entered a situation with preconceived ideas, and then had your ideas radically challenged or altered? Discuss what this process was like for you.
- How do you find yourself responding to those who disagree with your deeply held, personal convictions? How might your response shift when you focus on the sacred connection between you and another person?

Where Scarcity Meets Abundance

BY: TAYLOR PRYDE

I WAS ASKED TO be a scholarship reference for a young African-American man entering his senior year of high school. I was given the opportunity to tell the scholarship decision committee whether this young man met the "need" requirement to receive the scholarship. I checked each box that applied: works to support family: check, has experienced violence in immediate family: check, has housing insecurity: check, has food insecurity: check, has a family member in jail: check. I looked at the bottom of the recommendation for the space to talk about why I think this young man deserves a scholarship. It was nowhere to be found. He had been reduced to boxes to check. It did not matter who he was or what he had to offer, only that he was "needy" enough.

It broke my heart to see this young man reduced to his "neediness." He is an exceptional son to his mother. He loves his sister with extraordinary courage and vulnerability. I watched him receive a paycheck and immediately buy every other young person in the summer group a snack on a hot day. He was one of the most effective and kind leaders I have ever worked alongside. Yet, to the scholarship committee, they only cared that he was "needy."

There was no line on the form for me to talk about the ways I needed him. What I learned from him. The way my leadership and work experience benefited from the many gifts and talents I witnessed in him. I tell this story to illustrate that we have a problem in our churches and our communities. We are surrounded by systems that want to limit and boil people down to how much need they may have. There is a movement that shifts away from this thinking known as asset-based community development. Asset-based community development takes a community, observes and maps its assets (positive components of the community already present), and works to empower, connect, and enliven the community based on those assets. Ultimately, churches, non-profits, and community organizations are attempting to re-imagine how we address poverty and community growth by looking at assets (gifts, talents, skills) rather than deficits in a community.

Within the context of church, it means that we see every individual as worthy, beloved, and capable of enriching our church with their gifts and talents. This sometimes requires a holy reimagining. Society has taught us to prize certain gifts and talents over others. Jesus teaches us that even the bleeding woman is worth stopping in a crowd to listen to (Mark 5:24–35). Asset-based community development encourages us to see an elderly member of the church who bakes an incredible pound cake for her neighbor as a leader of hospitality, creativity, and generosity in the community rather than reducing her to a simple participant in the United Methodist Women's bake sale. We see her now as a leader and disciple while celebrating a gift that is already present in her life.

Asset-based community development encourages the church to ask the right questions. Rather than ask, what do you need, what can we do for you? We instead ask: Who are you? What makes you happy? If you could do anything in the world what would it be? When we ask these questions we see passion, love and abundance in places we previously had only seen "need." When we ask these questions often enough we start to see the abundance of connections and beauty in God's church and we are enlivened to empower and connect people to bring about the kingdom.

It is tempting for difficult conversations to begin with deficit. How can we meet the need? Whether that need is for inclusion of LGBTQA people or for the need to maintain dialogue between differences, we are rooted, still, in "need." What more can we do, what are we lacking, how can we survive? Instead of asking what can we do, we need to ask how we can be helped? Ask yourself, "in what ways can I be helped by someone who is different or believes something different than me?" This is a question that matters no matter if you are a progressive leaning congregation or a traditionalist leaning congregation. No matter who you are, we must be asking, what can we learn? what gifts can be offered from the other?

I believe the possibilities of mutual learning, growth, and celebration will be innumerable if we approach each interaction and relationship with the belief that everyone is a beloved child of God who has a gift. I had the opportunity to hear a classmate preach a sermon in which her own experience of coming out as queer informed her understanding of Jesus's own "coming out" as Savior to the universe. I needed that classmate's story to understand the isolation and rejection Jesus experienced. Her reading of scripture was informed by her experience as a queer woman. In the same way, I have worshiped in churches that advocate for a traditionalist approach. In those places, I have better learned who

Jesus is, the importance of church, and the power of community held within tradition. My understanding of Jesus and the church needs both ends of the spectrum.

Our understanding of Jesus is informed by the recognition of the gifts and assets brought forth by the full range of perspectives. We are also at risk of missing gifts and talents of all people when we do not choose to see each person as beloved and gift-filled. Despite political beliefs, sexual orientation, and gender identity, all people have gifts to offer your congregation. Making a stance that alienates any group of people means losing many gifts that enrich your community. You lose a beautiful voice from your choir, a gifted poet, a cook, a fisher, a teacher, a craftsperson, a landscaper, a farmer, a comedian, maybe even a beloved staff person in the church. Behind the titles and the positions, there are people who God deems beloved.

Broadway United Methodist Church in Indianapolis, Indiana, in many ways has pioneered asset-based community development in the church. At first glance it looks like this is entirely related to the ways in which they interact with the neighborhood surrounding the church. Much of the church work there is centered around believing and celebrating the gifts that are present in the low-income neighbors. This has resulted in a bustling community church that has jump-started catering companies for people, clay-working, an African dance studio, a children's orchestra and many more. This is a church that was surrounded by "need" but, instead, saw abundance.

This is only one half of the story for Broadway United Methodist Church. Broadway United Methodist Church is attended by a spectrum of individuals. From a ninety-nine year old member who was baptized in the church to a majority attendance of LGBTQA members. Despite the importance of sexuality and sexual identity of members, Broadway's beauty was much more about the way those individuals were celebrated. Broadway was a place that it wasn't about sexuality, it was about "Oh, you're a photographer. Can I see your portfolio? Maybe you can do family portraits for me." "Join the choir. We are happy to have you!" "I hear you like theatre; want to go to this play together?" By living into a community and a culture of abundance and celebration of gifts, it became possible for people to join together despite differences.

When we celebrate others and their gifts, we are celebrating God's image in the people we worship alongside. In times of fear, anxiety, uncertainty, and questioning we must seek God. I heard a prayer recently that said "we have a God who meets scarcity with abundance." This is a season in the United Methodist Church where it is so easy to see scarcity. Where we can be consumed by our anxiety and concern that we aren't doing enough, that we can't survive this disagreement. We instead have a God who fills those places of anxiety and scarcity with abundance. When we can lean into that abundance, we can be the church together.

<u>Discussion questions:</u>

- Share a story of some time you needed someone else and their differences were a gift to you.
- What are some ways we can center our community around the gifts of others rather than the needs of others?
- How does looking at the gifts of others change your perception of their differences?

Did He Just Say That? Friendship with My Neighbors

BY: RYAN KLINCK

"Did . . . he just say that?" My stomach drops, and my jaw clenches at the same time. My first instinct is to yell and interrupt him as my cheeks boil red, but fear simultaneously grabs ahold of my heart. "What if . . . " A million reasons why I should not engage what has been said flood into my mind. "He will get angry at me; I don't want to get yelled at; he doesn't know any better; no one else noticed it anyways, right?"

I decide to take the temperature of the room. Shelly glares daggers at him. "Oh dear, that is a fight waiting to happen." Eun Soo's mouth is agape, speechless. "I feel you brother." Angie appears confused. "Poor Angie . . . " Keith nods in agreement. "Of course, he agrees with him." My housemate glances back at me, eyebrows raised. "Yeah, he definitely said that." John carries on, oblivious to the impending eruption of responses of dissent and agreement that are about to burst upon him. "This could get ugly."

I am torn. I want to stand up for myself and name how what he said was hurtful, but I am also afraid. I do not want to be wounded even further. I take a deep breath and ask myself, "How should I respond to my friend? Friend . . . "

Whenever someone hurts, offends, or scares me, I tend to move into a space I like to call "survival mode," where I either want to fight or run away. In that space, I am not at my best. I am not my usual calm, peaceful, and open self who listens well; instead I am quick to judge, I push the other person away, and I make them into an enemy. I lose sight of the reality that the person who is in front of me is a human being who is likely to respond the same way I do whenever I hurt, offend, or scare them. I forget that Jesus asks me to do something preposterous in those "survival mode" moments; he asks me to love my enemy. The opposite of an enemy is a friend. If I am to love my enemy in that moment, then I need to treat them as my friend: their true identity. So, what is friendship? And how do I treat an other as my friend when every part of me being wants to treat them like an enemy?

For the past four years, I wrestled with these questions as I sought to build friendships with my neighbors in Old East Dallas. I lived at the Dietrich Bonhoeffer House, where three house residents and myself pray daily, follow a rule of life, and journey together with our neighborhood. Since the house's inception, we have provided a weekly community meal to connect with our neighbors: those who struggle with food security, homeless, low-income, disabled, and immigrant neighbors. Yet, over time, we noticed an unsettling trend; we were exhausted every time one of these neighbors came by for the meal, a shower, to do laundry, or grab a pair of socks. Every knock on the door led to a visible sigh and an internal feeling of dread. When we talked about how exhausted we were as a house, we hated how we felt because we loved the people we were journeying with, but we also did not know what to do about what we were experiencing.

One day, one of our house members finally named what we all needed to hear. "Our relationships with our neighbors are not relationships. We say that those who come to our house are our friends, but they are entirely one-directional relationships.

Friendship, a true relationship, goes two ways." I felt like he had slapped my face. I did not want to believe that all our work to build connections with our neighbors had been so flawed. But, he was right. Even though we had broken down the physical walls of our home and welcomed our neighbors into our house, our invisible interior walls were still up. We had sat down at a table with our neighbor every week for a meal, yet we seldom sat down long enough to have a meaningful conversation with our "friends." We had prayed together with our neighbor, yet we failed to share our hearts and what was truly bothering us. Our assumption that we were to be providers for our neighbors' needs and our unconscious prejudices had kept us from forming authentic relationships with our friends and disempowered them. We had somehow forgotten that Jesus said to his disciples, "I do not call you servants any longer . . . I [call] you friends." (John 15:15) We had been excellent servants to our neighbors, but terrible friends.

So, we began to ask ourselves, "What does it mean, then, for us to have a mutual, two-way friendship with our neighbors? We realized that if we were going to be friends with our neighbors, we had to actually treat them like friends. We, as house members, had to release any notion that we were there to save our neighbors through our service. In our efforts to "serve" them, we had unknowingly dismissed their gifts and abilities, making it impossible for our neighbors to reciprocate their love for the house members. It was kind of like saying, "Hey, we know you are an awesome cook, but you aren't ever allowed to cook because we have to cook for you, even though we aren't as good at it as you are." We could no longer treat them as poor souls who could not contribute anything. That simply was not true. These were gifted, incredible people who wanted to participate and help us. Why not let them prepare the table, cook, clean the space, and lead prayers? Why not ask, "Frank, would you be willing to grab a few folks to set the table? I am cooking tonight and my hands are a bit full." Friends help friends all the time. We did not need to do everything.

Along with creating space for our neighbor's gifts, we had to learn how to be vulnerable and honest with them about our own struggles. Friendship required us to accept the reality that we were not super-humans who could save the day, but simply human beings who had needs and problems just like our neighbors. We needed space to be listened to, and we needed to share about how drained we felt. To our surprise, our neighbors were great listeners. We simply had refused to believe that they would listen to us and hear our struggle. Slowly, we learned that we needed our neighbors' friendships just as much as they needed ours. Eventually, we could accept that our friends cared deeply about us and longed to know how they could pray for us. Finally, with time and courage we could ask, "Alonzo, when you talked about your family earlier, it reminded me that I am struggling with my relationship with my father right now. Can you pray for me?"

While we learned how to be better friends as house members, there were times when our neighbors chose not to act like friends, and they broke sacred boundaries. We had to learn to ask ourselves: "Do friends interrupt others during their prayer?" "Do friends take food from the fridge without permission?" "Do friends continue to sneak into our backyard to sleep at night when we have asked them to stop?" "How do we respond to our friend when they break our boundaries?" We had to learn how to hold our ground in a way that honored our friendships with our neighbors. Doing so is no small task. It takes guts to let your friend know when they have asked too much of you. "Hey Karen, could we meet at Starbucks and talk about this tomorrow? I had a really long day and am feeling a bit overwhelmed right now. I want to be able to listen to you well, but I need to be in a different head space to do so." It breaks your heart when you have to say, "Debbie, you know we love you, but you can't be here while you're drunk. It's not fair to everyone else. Let me grab you some food and water, and let's go sit outside together on the porch." It takes God's love to face a friend when they have hurt you and to say, "John, when you said that, it made me feel small and insignificant. As your friend, I want you to understand why. Can we talk about that together?"

Friendship is hard because people are messy. They do not fit into our preconceived categories. Real people are frustrating, fun, ornery, complicated, delightful, broken, quirky, impossible, and sacred gifts. They are bound to do things that drive us crazy, say things that we disagree with, and embody a life that disrupts our perceptions of how the world works. That is not a bad thing. The women and men who come to Bonhoeffer House constantly challenge my unconscious prejudices about them and surprise me with their generosity, grace, and love for others. I need friends like that in my life. Friends who can save me from my isolated corner where I think I know what is right. Friends who invite me to come back to the holy middle, where we do not have to shout at a distance but can meet each other face to face. Friends who help me see God's image in each person who is right in front of me.

"Did . . . he just say that?" My heartbeat quickens as my mouth drops. My first instinct is to run over and join the conversation. John is carrying on again. All eyes are on him. He has said something provocative, though, when does he not? Yet, this time faces smile, eyes tear up, and hugs are given. He says to another, "You are my friend, and there is no way in hell that I am going to let my friend sleep outside in this weather tonight. You are coming over to my place after we finish up here."

<u>Discussion questions:</u>

- What happens inside of you whenever someone says or does something that offends, scares, or hurts you? How do you initially want to respond to someone when this happens?
- Think about your friends. What makes them your friends? What is a good friendship? Why is that friendship meaningful to you?
- How might assuming a posture of friendship help you respond to someone differently? What might you say to invite someone into deeper friendship?

Sacred Liminal Spaces

BY: ROSE OXLEY

WE FIND OURSELVES IN another strange moment of human history concerning the Church. We are evolving, once more, in theology and practice. Neglected and forgotten voices are rising up, standing on the legacy of those who shouted in the wilderness— for inclusion, and for justice. Through grace, gifts, and perseverance, these voices now find themselves in positions of change and of authority—itching to create something new and challenge the status quo which seeks to continue suppressing and neglecting them. I find myself cautiously, but boldly, among those voices, as a self-avowed queer woman with gifts and graces for the servanthood of ministry among the United Methodist people.

I joined the United Methodist Church in 2012 after a year of prayerful discernment, observation, and ministry participation. I fell in love with these people called United Methodists and desired to join their journey. Early on in my journey I discovered a strange familiarity and awakening through learning about our history, our worship structure, and our methodical sense of order regarding discipleship and social justice advocacy. It felt familiar, like a song I once heard but now know the words to, and I reveled in the seemingly inherent flexibility of it all. Services weren't monochromatic, but rich in content and theology. These services incorporate prayers, congregational response and participation, and hymns that tell stories and did not necessitate nor force emotional responses—though they often could. Eventually, I even took to dying my hair according to the liturgical calendar as a spiritual practice. I fell madly in love with our methodical nature regarding worship resourcefulness and observation.

Our methods, as flawed as our institution remains, serve as an inclusive means for incorporating congregational participation, providing a variety of resources, and encouraging flexibility in cultivating worship so that all those present can find something that speaks to them. I argue for the inclusive nature of our United Methodist worship styles and resources because structuring worship using the tools and resources of our hymnals, prayer books, and lectionary, invites others in who need more than just a song and sermon. These resources serve to intentionally engage those present rather than existing as a pseudo show-and-tell karaoke hour.

Before you think this essay is simply a rage against the machine of contemporary worship styles—though I do find it difficult to contain my bias—this essay's primary concern is to address the emerging sacred liminal spaces we find in worship. These spaces are newly forming in our worship life of the UMC—and going vastly ignored. As neglected voices find themselves in positions of leadership and organizational authority, new narratives and stories are being woven in to our litanies; our previously held practices are being challenged for not adapting as they are able for the sake of providing the truly inclusionary spaces they are adept to do.

My queer-self lives for traditional, and often even, more conservative worship practices—silence, fasting, prayer walks (labyrinth), Maundy Thursday foot washing services, and lectionary based liturgical observances. But for other traditionalists, I am too queer and therefore either not qualified or too sinful to construct, lead, and participate in worship for and with them. Likewise, I am far too much a traditionalist to find a presence of worship with my contemporary queer (radical) peers. I came to this realization during my last annual conference. I sat among a vast array of United Methodist Christians—rural, urban, queer, conservative, part-time, full-time, laity, youth, and retired. As we opened our sessions with worship and began organizing ourselves to attend to the business of the church, I found myself lost. Hymns, which bind us to our history and to the integrity of the United Methodist Church, were completely altered by tune, meter, and even language—we struggled to sing with one voice "Are We Yet Alive," as the praise band invited us to sing the classic in a new way . . . many like myself just stared at the screen while the praise band "Oooed" and "Aaahed" on the stage before us. I remember leaving frustrated and empty that afternoon. Later that same day, I met a WCA[36] member from a small rural church in Montana. I asked her if she had been able to worship, or even be prayerfully present, during our moments of worship together. She responded simply and quietly, "no." My heart broke.

Annual Conferences are a unique and beautiful time for us to come together across geographic boundaries, socio-political preferences, and urban and rural ministry settings to engage as United Methodists—celebrating the best of us and creating a protective but vulnerable enough space for the worst of us. I quickly realized that not only was I not alone in my own lack of spiritual engagement, but something interesting and frustrating was happening. In real time, I experienced the tangible divide

---

36 Wesley Covenant Association

in the room as our moments of worship became a tool to shut down, shut out, and exclude "the other." And in that space, the "other" was everyone not a member of the LGBTQIA community or our ally. Our liturgies explicitly called out solidarity with queer members of our United Methodist Church, our hymns were so overtly altered that long-standing United Methodist members could not follow the tune nor the meter leaving them (and myself) attending a concert rather than a service. In this space, even as a queer woman, I stood appalled. As I understand my membership and ties to the United Methodist Church, the point is for me to fit in, not stand out and become a beacon or focal point for soap box moments like the ones I experienced during my last conference. Because, if we cannot even worship together, without elevating some of us over the rest of us, then we are not doing our ministry, our church, or ourselves any justice.

Our gatherings, whether they occur during worship in a local church setting, or at an annual conference session, ought to display a representative example of the diversity found within these places—upholding the best within us, and granting space for vulnerability, serving as beacons for inclusion, and dynamic disciple-making. They should also be spaces where we offer a grace-filled world of dissent which is grounded in grace and love. Instead of an "either/or" world, we ought to embrace the possibility of a "both/and" world. In other words, our gathering spaces, whether they be during our annual conference, or amidst the nature of our local churches, must create spaces of awareness with and for one another. This does not mean that we can pick and choose which group or voice we will elevate. If we truly declare ourselves to live in a gospel of liberation, then we must live into a gospel of liberation for all persons, with no one group or voice upheld over the other—even if that voice is a marginalized or oppressed faction of our society.

Living in a "both/and" world presents us the freedom to build bridges without demanding any one side to jump the chasm in order to meet "us" where we are. As a queer woman with traditional theological tendencies and practices, I find myself existing in a liminal space of moderation. I am too queer for my conservative and (often) rural peers, and too traditional for my radical queer peers. I do not quite fit in either world of worship, but I am called to be in both as I hold dear the aspects of both. Many of my queer siblings assert the only way to true liberation is to burn down the institution and begin anew. However, I fail to see the inclusivity in a process like that. Why reinvent the wheel when one can adapt the wheel to fit different contexts and situations? Perhaps this reasoning is why I tend to lean towards a more traditional and resource-based form of worship and practice. I love having spaces and systems to play around with—using what has been, and attempting to reshape it instead of establishing an entirely new structure crafted for only one voice or one style. My queer siblings, and our allies, are crafting beautiful forms of worship for the broken and forgotten members of our community who have been exiled from church and from religious institutions—this is necessary and fruitful work. However, when members of the church establish entire worship spaces for a single group of persons—like reconciling congregations, who promote their inclusivity above their United Methodist identity or desire to make disciples of Jesus Christ for the transformation of the world—while members outside of those select groups are present, they often serve to harm and exclude. In other words, in much of the reshaping being done, radical progressive members of our body are using worship and worship spaces to feed into the "us/them" dichotomy they claim to despise and combat.

I wonder whether we are enforcing silos of individual groups through spaces of grief and desperation. Our incorporation of previously manipulated, neglected, and even ignored narratives and voices into the greater establishment and practiced forms of worship is necessary for liberation. Stories from marginalized people serve as vital and crucial methods for primary sources and reshaping interpretations of litanies, language used, and forms of worship resources once recited without doubt or question. It is important that the church celebrate these narratives as the people telling them feel more comfortable, more emboldened, and more free to share them. But it is not celebration when these narratives become the only voice we elevate. This is a different kind of homogeneity, and it will lead us from one echo chamber to another. Over time, this echo chamber will consume us, if it hasn't begun to already.

There exists a grace, inherent in our gathering together, where worship leaders and organizational committees provide a space that does not influence nor coerce a preference of one form of worship or participation over another. This grace extends itself across the diverse range of persons in the room when not one voice stands out. Even though the diverse range of who we are and what we believe varies, we cannot allow ourselves to revert to existing oppressive power structures. A marginalized group plays into existing oppression when they hold the seat of power and continue the cycle towards their former oppressors. How? By using their platform to craft worship spaces for the ears of a single group of persons. While we desperately need these voices and these experiments with worship spaces, we cannot allow ourselves to go so far into the new without leaving breadcrumbs behind, something familiar, for those not able nor prepared to make the leap.

Cultivating sacred liminal spaces for worship is a beautiful means of literally bridging the gap in a sacred space where all can be present. Instead of either side looking across the chasm and demanding the "other" jump, we can recraft our resources and worship styles to be intentionally inviting—breadcrumbs from the familiar into the building blocks of the new and liberated. Instead of speaking out of grief, fear, and justified retaliation, we have an opportunity before us during this exciting shift of church history, to establish vulnerable spaces for the moderate liminal people like myself. We can present styles and resources that reinvent what binds us together with more intentional language for inclusion while upholding the sacred nature of congregational participation and a liturgical structure. We must live into a communion with one another. For, all who seek Christ and desire forgiveness of their sin are welcome at this table. Why, then, must we continue erecting walls in such holy spaces of grace?

Discussion questions:

- How does building bridges with common ground so that "both sides" may have materials and resources to be present help us know our communities?
- How can reading commentaries from marginalized voices and incorporating them into our conversations, sermons, and litany inform our worship practices?
- How do practices of consideration lead to better disciple-making, living into liberation for all, involving the dirty work of reconstructing . . . not burning the whole institutional structure down?

5

Encountering the Self

BY: ANDREA LINGLE

I do not understand my own actions. For I do not do what I want, but I do the very thing I hate.

Romans 7:15

"Ask, and it will be given to you; search, and you will find; knock, and the door will be opened for you. For everyone who asks receives, and everyone who searches finds, and for everyone who knocks, the door will be opened."

Matthew 7:7,8

PEOPLE ARE WEIRD. FROM Oedipus to Kanye, we live among irrational, emotional, frustrating people. When two people are having a disagreement, it is fair to say there are at least six people in that disagreement. Who you are, who you think you are, who they think you are, who they are, who they think they are, and who you think they are. Suddenly, the general chaos of governments, corporations, and churches makes more sense. How are we to ever bridge ideological chasms when everyone who enters the room triples the possible chaos of the system?

In the Gospel of Matthew, chapter 7, Jesus is teaching about trying to live civilly. How to be the Community of God in a kind way. The chapter opens with the familiar injunction not to judge "lest ye be judged," then you get the bit about the log in your own eye, and then a picturesque, if dramatic, warning about not giving pearls to swine. Of course there are so many good lessons in that, but these are all about how to constrain our natural tendency to avoid dealing with our self.

Looking to the other for a reference for what our behavior should be is as old as time and children.

"Why did you color on the wall?"
"[Name of sibling] was doing it!!"
"Why did you hit [your sibling]?"
"[He/She/It/They] kicked me right in the FACE."

It's the old everyone-else-is-doing-it bit, or the at-least-I'm-not-doing-*that* bit. But Jesus must have known what Alcoholics Anonymous has learned: healing begins with acknowledging the self. "Hi, my name is Andrea, and I am addicted to control."

But how? Constraining the self does not usually lead to life-long change. Looking at you, Low-fat Diet. Jesus said, the one who asks will find the answers, the one who seeks will find. Perhaps, the understanding we need to sit at a difficult table is found, not in the answers we receive, but in the process of questioning what we do and why.

Sometimes the reason that we cannot have difficult conversations is that we don't know who and what WE bring to the table. Until we take the time to ask and seek who we are, we will remain at the mercy of our unconscious triggers, unruly, emotions, and unexamined insecurities. After all, Jesus said to love our neighbor as we love ourselves.

THE GATHERING

Words of Gathering

Gather all participants in the eating space and read these words aloud together:

God in Community,

We gather today as a sign that we are willing to engage in the work of community. We acknowledge that we have come with our selves, our pasts, and our fears. Give us the courage to inhabit this place in a holy way.

Setting the Table

Setting the table is an act of radical intention. It is making room for each participant—for their needs, experiences, and desires. Set the table as a community, being mindful of each person whose place is being laid. As each place is laid, these words of commitment may be offered:

Spirit of Grace, may [participant's name] be met with grace, held in respect, and guided toward wisdom.

When the table is set, gather the group around the table and share this blessing (the blessing can be read responsively or as a group):

Table Blessing

For the heartbreak I carry, **we pray**
For the heaviness within me
that yearns to connect
For the grief that I carry
For the ways that I've tried
We give thanks

For the ways I've not listened
For the judgments I've leapt to
For assumptions I've made
We forgive you

I am here
I am still trying
Among the rest
Together, we hold our heav
ness and our efforts with
honor and care

May we find at this table
a grace that helps us
Stand
Sit
Remain
Pray
And listen

May we be patient
have compassion for
ourselves
We are here
We are trying
We are held in the infinite
grace and mercy of
The God who abides
The Spirit who enlivens
The Jesus who forgives

Thank you, fellow strugglers
For your presence
Thank you for honoring mine

We are here and we are
trying

May this space at the table
knit us together.
Amen.

Breaking Bread

After the food is served, have one of the participants read the following:

> *By gathering around this table, we intend to listen to the stories of the other. We will not use words or gestures to harm. If conflict arises, we will remember that it is the work of this space to engage in holy conflict. We commit to holding the personhood of the other as precious.*
>
> **Amen.**

As you begin eating, notice any tension and awkwardness in the area. Allow it to be present. Notice how the conversation rises. Notice the passing of the food. After the meal is underway, begin the practice.

A Practice of Drumming
BY: WENDI BERNAU

Preparation:

A drum circle is an organic, dynamic community conversation of rhythm rather than words. Participants should be made aware that they will be participating in a practice of contemplative meditation and should be prepared to offer at least ten minutes to a very repetitive activity. There is no talking during the drumming; some people may experience boredom if they have not practiced meditation previously. Encourage these participants to give themselves to the process for the benefit of the group. There are only two rules to drum circle participation:

Be present

Play along

In the circle, the simple heartbeat gradually becomes a more complex system that changes as participants offer new sounds to the group. There are no soloists and no one needs to self-identify as a musician to participate. Everyone is welcome. A multitude of sounds can be achieved with simple body percussion: tapping on a table with fingers, patting on one's lap, clapping hands, snapping fingers; tapping, shuffling or stomping feet. Participants are encouraged to discover and add new sounds as they are comfortable, ready, and willing.

Drum circle participants, in the process of listening and tapping, are ideally entering a state called entrainment. When the drummers are fully engaged and in sync with one another, playing the rhythms becomes an effortless release of thought and they can enter a meditative state where the sound becomes an energy rather than a collection of noises. Participants experience a feeling of unity with the group when this happens. Drum circle leaders listen attentively to that energy, can feel the energy shift and know when the conversation is at a peak and when it has subsided. A common mistake for beginners is to end the drumming too early, before everyone has found the courage to let go of their inhibitions and fully engage with the group's rhythm or try new sounds. It typically takes about ten minutes for a group to go through the cycle.

The Activity

To begin, choose one person to start the seed rhythm and be the timekeeper. This person will continue to pat a steady beat like the ticking of a clock for the duration of the exercise and also will end the drumming after approximately ten minutes, when it feels like the momentum has peaked and settled again.

As they are ready, the other participants join the patting with their own rhythm, listening to and keeping within the overall sound of the group. At first, this may feel awkward and it may take five or more minutes for everyone to feel comfortable enough to try a new rhythm or sound. The group will ideally foster a safe and inviting atmosphere for these new sounds. The seed rhythm player may change the seed to a more complicated rhythm, but if the group starts to break apart, the seed player is responsible for bringing a steady beat back.

After the ten minutes and when it feels like the group's energy has diminished, the seed rhythm player will end the drumming by counting aloud on the beats backward from five, so that all end together.

<u>Questions for Reflection:</u>

Allow a few moments for participants to silently consider the experience, then discuss the following questions:

- What was this experience like for you?
- How did you begin to enter into this experience?
- How did your experience change over the course of the drumming?
- Was there a moment of high energy? How did that feel?
- What did you notice about the group as you were drumming? About yourself?
- How was this experience similar and different to having a conversation with words?

Discussion

Use the discussion questions at the end of the selected essay to guide a discussion.

Reflection

As the meal ends, take a moment to reflect. If it is helpful, one participant can read these questions aloud:

- What about this discussion encourages me?
- What about this discussion makes me angry? Why?
- What can I learn about myself?
- What have I heard? What have I refused to hear?

Clearing the Space

After the reflection is over, all participants will work together to clear the table, wash the dishes, sweep the floor, and return the space to order. This is done to symbolize that even through conflict, we are committed to compassion, grace, and peace.

After the eating space is returned to order, gather for a closing benediction.

Words of Benediction

Ever present God, we devote ourselves to the covenant of Love that Your Son established on Earth— may we serve you and love our neighbor as ourselves with the unadulterated love you bestow unto us.

We seek deep for answers. We explore the vast spaces of our being.

Let us be in constant awe of the wonder that we are—wholly loved, and wholly incredible.

Amen.

ESSAYS

Unexpected. Interrupted.

BY: KATEY RUDD

It's 12:00pm:

I'm finally sitting down to return overdue emails, write a nearly overdue article, and slog through a grant outline. Maybe I'll have time to get part of one of these tasks done in the hour I don't have anything planned today and can simultaneously inhale a sandwich. I thought I'd be able to do some of this before our 9:00am team meeting but chicken care and watering seedlings for our garden took longer than I thought this morning, so I'm starting now.

It's 12:07pm:

(Hears door open.) A neighbor is here and has a question, needs space held, wants to feel connected.

This takes thirty-ish minutes.

Success!: We had a fantastic talk. Our neighbor left being more a part of what we are collaboratively creating here at Haw Creek Commons. I am more connected to them.

NOT success: My emails, article, grant outline.

This may happen five more times today if I stay present in this space.

I am committed to being present. But now I'm pressured. Now I haven't eaten, feel doubly behind, have a meeting in fifteen minutes, and am hoping to have a semblance of a personal life tonight without dropping too many balls. How do I feel? Stressed. Anxious. Frustrated. Overwhelmed. I start to punitively calculate the "lost" minutes in my head with a grrrr in the back of my throat even though I know the time I just spent in relationship is the whole point of what we are doing. I wonder how I can get it all done.

I think we've all been here no matter how much we care about people. We need to be calm, competent, spiritual, hold space, facilitate community without injecting anxiety, restlessness or being short with people.

I don't want to pretend to be this. I want to BE this. It has to be real. If it's not real than our message is just another game and I don't want to be a salesman. If we can't genuinely be in community with grace our community will reflect that. As leaders, we set the tone, hopefully a spacious tone. We cannot have narrative that has no backbone.

All of us, staff and friends at Missional Wisdom Foundation, are strange enough to place ourselves in this position every day, all day, because we have this wild vision that community itself is a means of grace. This sounds fantastic as an outward theology, that creating community opens an avenue for people to experience God, each other, and the world, no evangelical agenda required or desired.

The real kicker is this theology absolutely demands dedication to an inward practice of patience, grace, listening, and humility before community even hits the scene.

Our collective goal is to create a container for community to create itself. Easier said than done. There are myriad variables. This theology only has power if it effectively bears an ecology. (**Ecology**: *The set of relationships existing between any complex system and its surroundings or environment.*) Our theology in our contextualized ecology must be translated to momentary practice that has no end point for community to become our culture. We make space for the unexpected. We make space for the interruption. We don't TRY, we ARE present.

Grace doesn't come easily or permanently between humans. We have to plan for it and practice it. We have to cycle forgiveness and resilience when things hurt us or afront our ideal. We have to communicate. Grace happens when we get out of books and heady conversation then hit the dirty pavement of daily community. It gets practical quickly. It gets personal even quicker because it's about our *schedule*.

No matter how you slice it, our schedules and particularities are about *us*. It's natural. It's where we are in control and create our own comfort. What if we rearrange our schedule to be a commons schedule?

A few practices that have been helpful to me:

- Create a multi-day schedule for 3 days minimum
- Star the 4–7 most important tasks to be accomplished the day you write the list and do those that day, interruptions aside. (If you have large projects, break them into manageable task-sized steps to be included in this list.)
- Plan for 2–3 hours (or more) of "interruption" per day. **Consider those hours your greatest work.**
- Take care of yourself, every day, however that looks.
- Practice Sabbath. As Wendell Berry says, "Practice Resurrection." (Manifesto: The Mad Farmer Liberation Front, *poem*)

Discussion questions:

- How do we spend our time?
- What are we creating in that time?
- WHY do we spend our time that way and to what end?
- What does it look like to have a community-centered approach to our daily life while still maintaining people-centered, self-sustaining businesses and projects that demand definitive outcomes (all while staying sane and healthy?)
- MOST IMPORTANTLY: What do we consider "interruption?" Is our definition accurate? How does expanding or contracting our perspective affect our capacity to be present in our communities and lead a culture of grace?

The Dance

BY: DARRYL DAYSON

"I want to learn how to hold the paradoxical poles of my identity together, to embrace the profoundly opposite truths that my sense of self is deeply dependent on others dancing with me and that I still have a sense of self when no one wants to dance."[37]
Parker Palmer

ONE OF MY FAVORITE guilty pleasures is the competition show "So You Think You Can Dance." Yes, week after week, I live vicariously through dancers who have committed themselves to the art of movement and put their talents on display, but more importantly, I see them grow by being emotionally, physically, and, at times, spiritually stretched as they learn genres and the ebb and flow of their partners.

Dance is such a beautiful art. You can watch a dancer do a solo piece as an expression of themselves. While they fly through the air, contort their bodies, and pirouette, we learn something about who that person is. Then, when they are asked to partner and dance with someone else, we become more familiar with who they are. Each person has to have an awareness of their own strengths and weaknesses. When you think about a dancer leaping into the arms of another, you can't help but think about their vulnerability as they land in the arms of their partner. Each individual has to communicate their past injuries, comfortability with particular

---

37 Palmer, *The Courage to Teach*, 75.

styles, and their preference in movement. To be an accomplished dancer you have to work for it.

During one of the clips of the grueling process of learning and practicing new group choreography, the leading instructor, Mandy Moore, saw the exhaustion of the dancers as they mumbled under breaths and were hunched over with hands on their knees, and pepped them up by saying, "This is dance, it's hard."

Diving into conversations that we know can cause tension, anxiety, and pain is hard. I dare say it can be as difficult, if not more, than dance. To enter into sacred spaces and have holy conversations about matters that are personal and vulnerable, we must first come into those places and spaces acknowledging our own stories.

Knowing oneself requires hard work. It calls us to introspection and reflection, to learn, know, and claim our own stories. When we know ourselves and become comfortable in our own skin and stories, we are then able to open ourselves to others more intimately and vulnerably.

Oddly enough, doing the work to know oneself should not be done in isolation. Self-examination and introspection is most healthfully done in the midst of intimate and vulnerable communal interactions with people you know and trust. This work of knowing must be done within community and with God. It is by God's grace that we are brought into community together, and it's by the work of the Holy Spirit that we are able to live in relationship with one another.

God's grace enables us to see how we have been shaped by the loving care of our family and community. We can learn and see how these relationships have helped define our values, mold our character, and, at times, perhaps, have left us with scars. Through spending time with our families and friends we begin to learn our story, through our study of scripture we learn the ancient stories of God's interactions with the world, and all of these strands weave together to form and shape who we are.

In this we also become more attuned to the ways how and who we are affects our relationship with our communities. We come to grips with how the ways we relate to one another at times can instigate the pain of separation and broken relationships. Grace then invites us to grow in our love for God, our community, and ourselves by shifting how we verbally and physically communicate with them.

Just as the Proverb says, "one person sharpens . . . another,"[38] through our relationships we can learn more about ourselves then we can learn on our own. One may be a gifted orator, but to engage in meaningful and vulnerable conversations with friends, family, and neighbors, it requires us to first do the work we need to do to understand and encounter ourselves. We must do this work so we may know how to make room for others in our lives and communities.

This process is akin to a divine dance. Like the Father, Son, and Holy Spirit, we are tasked with creating a place for mutual flourishing for those we are in community with by maintaining our unique personhood and engaging in the reciprocal act of leading and being led by the other. These interactions take a lot of rehearsal and choreography, but when they are practiced we have the opportunity to more fully connect with each other. Brené Brown defines this connection as "the energy that exists between

---

38 Proverbs 27:17

people when they feel seen, heard, and valued; when they can give and receive without judgment; and when they derive sustenance and strength from the relationship."[39]

Connecting with and encountering ourselves opens us to intimate connections with our communities that can help us be molded and shaped by one another into something more beautiful than when we are alone.

---

39 Brown, *The Gifts of Imperfection, 19.*

Discussion questions:

- Why is connecting with the self so hard?
- How is the life of faith like a dance?
- Like dance, community "is hard." How does being willing to explore who you are in community help you be a better community partner?

A Failure of the Heart

BY: KATHRYN HUNTER

I<small>T WAS A FAILURE</small> of the heart. We cared more for our stances than we did for our stories. We knew where we stood rather than who we were. I was the pastor of a church which fell apart under the pressures of conflict. I failed. I say that with humility but also with the knowledge that many of us, clergy and laity, fail to live peacefully in the face of conflict. We not only fail to find a solution—we fail to love one another.

We were a small, rural, church. We had sung "Blest Be the Tie that Binds" many times. We loved one another, after all most of the congregation was family, until the "others" began moving into the neighborhood. It was a shock to suddenly realize there were folks on the same pews who did not think like we had always thought!

The newer folks were looking for a church like they had attended in other places. Churches that provided many programs, missions, and a variety of worship styles. The long-time members wanted to stay a small rural church with no changes in style or in leadership. Unfortunately, we became a church of two sides. Each judged the other over everything—the clothes they wore, the pictures on the walls in the church, the way to do Sunday School, and, most of all, how to worship.

The Bible, and Jesus, are pretty clear on the issue of judging. We are not to judge one another. Read Romans 14:1–4 from the Message paraphrase:

Welcome with open arms fellow believers who don't see things the way you do. And don't jump all over them every time they do or say something you don't agree with—even when it seems that they are strong on opinions but weak in the faith department. Remember, they have their own history to deal with. Treat them gently.

For instance, a person who has been around for a while might well be convinced that he can eat anything on the table, while another, with a different background, might assume he should only be a vegetarian and eat accordingly. But since both are guests at Christ's table, wouldn't it be terribly rude if they fell to criticizing what the other ate or didn't eat? God, after all, invited them both to the table. Do you have any business crossing people off the guest list or interfering with God's welcome? If there are corrections to be made or manners to be learned, God can handle that without your help.[40]

In this passage, Paul was addressing a church made up of two very different cultures—Jewish Christians and Gentile Christians. The Jewish Christians were struggling with whether or not to continue to obey all of the Old Testament laws, including the dietary ones, where some meat was clean and some unclean. The Gentile Christians had never heard of those laws but did know that some meat sold in the marketplaces came from animal sacrifices to idols and wondered if it was okay to eat. The conflicts and

40 Peterson, *The Message Bible.*

struggles were over deeply held religious beliefs, and Paul advises the church—do not judge!

The twenty-first century church struggles over core issues of faith and understanding. Denominations struggle and, unfortunately, split over hard issues such as: homosexuality, abortion, immigration, and how scripture is to be understood. We disagree with those who share the pew with us.

So, back to my conflict fail-story. The anger and dissension got so bad within the church that, at the suggestion of our District Superintendent (DS), we hired counselors to work with the church in a process of mediation. Much to the church's credit they agreed to pay the cost and, mostly, they came and participated in and supported the process over several weeks.

The night came when we were to conclude the mediation process and work through the resolution of issues. It was a packed sanctuary. I wish that I could report a happy ending, that we had grown in love and came to a peaceful conclusion but that was not the case. Instead as we discussed our worship style dilemma, one person stood up and made a very judgmental, disrespectful comment, calling one of the worship services "a joke." It was all over. The Chair of Council threw up his hands and walked out and many people followed him out—never to return. It was a failure to love and respect one another. Judging builds the walls that keep us from truly knowing and loving one another.

Romans 14:4 says:

Who are you to judge someone else's servants? To their master, servants stand or fall. And they will stand, for the Lord is able to make them stand.

You and I are not called to judge our brothers and sisters.

They are God's servants and God will make them stand rightly before God.

Hear the grace in that! Even if I am wrong, God will help me stand—God will do any correcting that is necessary. We are called to love and not judge.

A few months after our disastrous meeting, I made the decision to request a change of appointment. As I talked with my District Superintendent, he asked me, "What would you have done differently?" I could only think of one thing; I wish there had been a way for the congregation to really get to know one another. At the time, that felt like a rather lame answer and I think, perhaps, the DS thought so too.

Now, years later, I know what I meant by that; if we could have been a people who were a part of each other's lives, if we had built relationships and listened and not judged, if we had done more sitting around the table and sharing our stories, I believe it could have been different. What a great church we could have been!

Through God's grace, that particular church still exists. They are still a part of the Body of Christ. They worship and they serve one another. New folks come and go. But God's grace is always present. Our sin does not win—God does!

The world desperately needs the church, the Body of Christ, to show God's love. The world needs the Body of Christ, to live together in unity and to be the hands and feet of Christ. The world desperately needs to see that peace is possible and that hope exists.

What a mighty witness to God's power, forgiveness, grace, and love when we, Christians, can love even in the midst of conflict.

Closing Prayer:

Living God, hear our prayers for one another. May we love as you love. Forgive us when we judge one another. Teach us to listen, to hear, to respect one another even when we may disagree. Help us to be instruments of peace and hope to a hurting world. In Christ's name, we pray. **Amen**.

Discussion questions:

- Have you ever been a part of a conflict within a church? Please share your feelings about that experience.
- It can be a painful experience to be judged, have you felt judged? How did you feel?
- Has there been a time in your life when your opinion of a person changed when you heard their story?

What is Mine to Do?

BY: ANDREA LINGLE

THERE IS A BUTTERFLY bush off the corner of my porch where I like to work. In summer, it is filled with cones of tiny white flowers. Each flower holds a tiny cup of nectar, sugar spun from the sun itself, to entice sextets of tiny, winged feet. As the butterflies, bees, and hummingbird moths[41] do their unintentional work of pollination, the flowers shrivel and turn brown, making way for the next phase of butterfly bush morphology. When I look at the whole bush, laden with hundreds of cones each made up of hundreds of flowers, the task of pollination seems impossible. How could the work ever get done?

But day by day, flutter by flutter, sip by sip, each flower gives the gift it holds and receives the pollen it needs, and by summer's end, the bush stands, with fingers denuded, accomplished and ready for fall. And the butterflies? They have gone, nourished, on their way. The work gets done, not because of the butterflies' force of will, but because they came to do what was theirs to do.

What is mine to do?

With more information than one human brain can assimilate at our fingertips, we run the risk of trying to pollinate every flower ourselves or, worse, bumble into situations we have not paused to understand—seeing the flowers fading to brown, we

---

41 These are real, and the name is a perfect descriptor. I discovered them three years ago when I moved to this house/porch/bush, and they still delight me.

assume, not that they are doing their work in the world but that they are dying and we should try to save them.

In our communities, we must learn to ask, "What is mine to do?"

There is more hurt, chaos, injustice, and conflict in the world than there are flowers on my bush, and that can feel overwhelming. Surely, someone should be doing something. And, yes, someone should be doing something. You should be doing something. But you can not be doing everything. You should be doing what is yours to do. I should be doing what is mine to do. The butterfly bush teaches us three reasons this is important. First, there is too much work for one insect to do. Second, there are many kinds of work to be done. There are dozens of kinds of pollinators on this bush. Not all of them are serving the same function (probably). And lastly, what would you call a butterfly who visited every flower? A hoarder, a glutton, a miser? There is nourishment to be had when going about the work to be done in the world. If we insist that all the work is ours, even if it were all possible for us to do (which it isn't), we would be hoarding the co-creation of the world.

What?

When God created humankind in God's own image, God created us to be creators. God created us to continue creating, along with God. God invited humankind into a collaborative song wherein we get to share not just our voice, but our creativity. When we decide that this is mine to do and this and this AND THIS, we deny the *imago dei* of the other.

Just as each flower holds nectar, each of us is met with sweetness in our work. It is manna. Bread for the day. Eucharist for the moment. Just enough to feed our souls for this moment, this hour, this day. But, if I take your work, I am robbing you of the nectar of that work.

So, we ask, what is mine to do?

Have you been to the grocery store in the United States of America lately? Have you been to the aisle with tomato sauce? You know, the aisle with the jar of tomato sauce that you would open and mix with ground beef, ground turkey, or sautéed broccoli, depending on your preference, if you needed to make dinner in the time it takes to boil a pot of water and cook pasta (7–8 minutes)? That aisle. Well, that aisle has about six thousand choices. I remember, shortly after delivering one of my babies, standing on that aisle, too exhausted to parse out the choices, frozen.

Sometimes what is ours to do seems like trying to decipher the difference between sweet basil and onion and chunky ragù. How do you ever decide? And when do you know when it is enough?

Well, I don't know.

The thinker in me wants to drown the answer in jargon, the mother in me wants to encourage (lecture) the asker, and the soul in me whispers . . . trust.

Because, I think, that is what this question comes down to: trust. Trusting that you are not required to do it all or know it all because you are part of a Community of God, and this community is wise.

The prophet Micah answered the question this way:

He has told you, O mortal, what is good;
and what does the Lord require of you

but to do justice, and to love kindness,
and to walk humbly with your God?
Micah 6:8

While I usually hate using "top ten verses," this one says something profound about life and bushes and God. We are required, by the Divine Creator, to do what is right, value what is kind, and walk, simply, unassumingly, trustingly, with God.

I am reminded that Dr. Elaine A. Heath teaches a simple way to do what's yours to do. In a book that she co-wrote with Larry Duggins, Dr. Heath, says,

> None of us can love as Jesus loves unless we are filled with the Holy Spirit. And this requires a day by day opening of ourselves to the love of God. It means we have to be born again, born of the Spirit.
>
> It means we have to live in a contemplative stance.
>
> To be a contemplative is to show up, pay attention, cooperate with God, and release the outcome.[42]

That's it. That's all. That is what is ours to do.

But wait, you say, what if there is that which I can do that is not being done. What if I see something that I think is wrong, and I know I can fix it. Does that make it mine to do? Perhaps. Perhaps not.

Going back to a bush, a different bush, a different time: a burning bush.

---

42 Heath and Duggins, *Missional. Monastic. Mainline.*, 29.

Moses was keeping the flock of his father-in-law Jethro, the priest of Midian; he led his flock beyond the wilderness, and came to Horeb, the mountain of God. There the angel of the Lord appeared to him in a flame of fire out of a bush; he looked, and the bush was blazing, yet it was not consumed. Then Moses said, "I must turn aside and look at this great sight, and see why the bush is not burned up." When the Lord saw that he had turned aside to see, God called to him out of the bush, "Moses, Moses!"

Exodus 3:1–4a

So, Moses was doing what was his to do. He was a shepherd. For his father-in-law. No more a prince of Egypt (after a small incident wherein he decided to do something it was probably not his to do), Moses was a desert shepherd of a borrowed flock. But one day, he went beyond the wilderness. What? Beyond the confusion? Beyond the given-up-ness of life? Beyond the stuckness? He went beyond all of those things toward the mountain of the Lord. And he looked. And he was curious, and he turned aside.

And that was when God noticed. Moses noticed and then God noticed, and then God spoke Moses's name. When was it Moses's to do? When he pushed past the wilderness, noticed the bush burning, and turned aside.

How do we know what is ours to do in the world? We don't. But we can follow our curiosity, listen to the Spirit, and let go of the rest.

Discussion questions:

- How do you know what is yours to do?
- How does the contemplative stance give you space to let go of what other people are doing?
- What are you co-creating in the world?

6

Committing to Grace

BY: ANDREA LINGLE

Here we are. Gathered again. It is been a journey of growth, but the work does not stop here, in fact it starts here. In Alexander Shaia's book *Heart and Mind*, he says:

> When "apostle" is used, it means "one who is sent out." "Disciple," however, is always applied in the context of "learner," and is always used when Jesus is teaching . . . the opportunity for apostleship comes with maturity, and yet discipleship—even for apostles—never ends. The spiritual journey will always require "continuing education" in how to offer wisdom appropriately and with compassion.[43]

---

43 Shaia, *Heart and Mind*, 329.

What we have learned along this way will serve to inform how we live in the world. The conflict we encounter. The spaces we create and inhabit. The work here is the work of grace. We must commit ourselves to the persistent task of loving deeply, risking courageously, and allowing grace to flow to and through our lives.

We have made a commitment to stay at the table during conflict, and we must now leave, committing, not to conflict, but to grace. May grace, the wild wanderer that laces our lives with mystery, hope, and courage, so fill us that the crumbs under our tables feed a thousand hungry souls.

THE GATHERING

Words of Gathering

Gather all participants in the eating space and read these words aloud together:

God in Community,

We gather today as a sign that we are willing to engage in the work of community. We acknowledge that we have come with our selves, our pasts, and our fears. Give us the courage to inhabit this place in a holy way.

Setting the Table

Setting the table is an act of radical intention. It is making room for each participant—for their needs, experiences, and desires. Set the table as a community, being mindful of each person whose place is being laid. As each place is laid, these words of commitment may be offered:

Spirit of Grace, may [participant's name] be met with grace, held in respect, and guided toward wisdom.

When the table is set, gather the group around the table and share this blessing (the blessing can be read responsively or as a group):

Table Blessing

For the strength within us, **we pray**

For remaining present
Remaining open
For our listening and our courage
We give thanks

For the creativity and resilience
To navigate a way forward
We ask for guidance

For facing the unknown
For holding space
For embracing the uncertainty

We grope in the darkness
May our table be woven in grace

May we have compassion
for our faults
Witness each other's
stories
Befriend failure and fear,
Receive their wisdom
Give us the strength to
craft peace and practice
love

May this space at the table knit us together.
Amen.

Breaking Bread

After the food is served, have one of the participants read the following:

> *By gathering around this table, we intend to listen to the stories of the other. We will not use words or gestures to harm. If conflict arises, we will remember that it is the work of this space to engage in holy conflict. We commit to holding the personhood of the other as precious.*
> **Amen.**

As you begin eating, notice any tension and awkwardness in the area. Allow it to be present. Notice how the conversation rises. Notice the passing of the food. After the meal is underway, begin the practice.

A Practice of Meditation
BY: WENDI BERNAU

Preparation:

When we find ourselves stuck in conflict and negativity, often with another person as the target of our distaste and venom, contemplative prayer and guided meditation can help to ease the soul and dissipate the anger. If we are filled with love, we cannot find room for hate.

In this exercise, the facilitator will lead the group through a guided meditation while participants envision and take on a posture of an ever-widening circle of love, grace and peace.

The Activity

Participants are invited to spread out around the room, making space for one another. Each person may choose to keep eyes open or closed, sit or stand, as they are comfortable.

Facilitator will lead participants through the following guided meditation, pausing between sentences, reading slowly and deliberately through the meditation:

> Take a few moments to breathe deeply. *(breathe with them, slowly and deliberately)*

> Notice any tightness in your body and relax your muscles, beginning with your neck and moving

to your shoulders, torso, stomach, legs and feet. *(breathe)*

Continue to breathe. If your thoughts wander, let them go. Release any desire to judge your own thoughts and come back to focus on your breathing. *(breathe)*

Think about a close, loving relationship with a person either living or deceased. This should be someone dearly beloved. See that person in your mind's eye and feel the deep affection you have for that person. Notice how this feels in your body. Allow your body to take the shape or posture of that feeling. Feel free to use your arms or legs as well as your hands. Feel the love you have for that person as you continue to breathe. *(breathe, give them a few moments to find a posture)*

Expand that circle to include your family and close friends. Extend the same feelings of love to each person. Picture these people in your mind's eye and offer the same love and affection that you hold for your beloved. Notice how this feels in your body and allow your body to take the shape or posture of that expanding circle of love and grace. Feel the love and grace as you continue to breathe. *(breathe, give them a moment to find a posture)*

Continue to expand the circle of love and grace to your acquaintances. Draw upon the intense love for your beloved and extend that same affection toward the larger community. Include those you don't know well. Picture one or more of these people in your mind's eye and offer the same love and affection that you hold for your beloved. Take on the posture of this expansion. Continue to feel the love, grace, and peace as you continue to breathe. *(breathe, give them a moment to find a posture)*

Expand the circle even further. From the same source as the affection for your beloved . . . extend the love, grace and peace to your circle of family and friends . . . outward to nominal acquaintances . . . and now expand even more to include those with whom you disagree, those with whom you are in conflict. Extend the same love to the person in conflict that you hold for the dear one. Picture that person in your mind and offer the same love and affection that you hold for your beloved. Envelop that person or persons in grace and peace. Notice how this feels in your body and take on that posture with your body. Continue to draw upon love, grace and peace as you continue to breathe. *(breathe, and give them a moment for them to find a posture. Note to facilitator: this exercise may make some people uncomfortable.*

Be sensitive to the participants and bring the exercise to a gentle close.)

Imagine now taking all of these people in the ever-widening circle and placing them all in the hands of God. Offer up to God all of the feelings that have emerged during this exercise. Release any tension as you breathe. When you are ready, release the final posture, breathe, and shake out your arms and legs to clear the space. *(breathe and wait for participants to finish)*

<u>Questions for Reflection:</u>

Allow a few moments for participants to silently consider the experience, then discuss the following questions:

- What was this experience like for you?
- What resistance did you experience? Why?
- Talk about the postures you took on. What connection do they have to your experience?
- What surprised you during this meditation?
- What did you learn about yourself during this meditation?
- How did it feel to extend the same love to the person of conflict that you hold for your beloved?

Discussion

Use the discussion questions at the end of the selected essay to guide a discussion.

Reflection

As the meal ends, take a moment to reflect. If it is helpful, one participant can read these questions aloud:

- What about this discussion encourages me?
- What about this discussion makes me angry? Why?
- What can I learn about myself?
- What have I heard? What have I refused to hear?

Clearing the Space

After the reflection is over, all participants will work together to clear the table, wash the dishes, sweep the floor, and return the space to order. This is done to symbolize that even through conflict, we are committed to compassion, grace, and peace.

After the eating space is returned to order, gather for a closing benediction.

Words of Benediction

Give us the courage to seek peace with one another and truly build a beloved community. **God we commit ourselves to live into your Peace.**

Give us humility to reach across boundaries and divisions. **God, we ask for grace-filled dissent so that we may celebrate our voices and talents.**

Ever present God, we devote ourselves to the covenant of Love that Your Son established on Earth—**may we serve you and love our neighbor as ourselves with the unadulterated love you bestow unto us. Amen.**

ESSAYS

The Practice of Love

BY: SARAH S. HOWELL-MILLER

*When the Son of Man comes in his glory, and all the angels
with him, then he will sit on the throne of his glory. All the
nations will be gathered before him, and he will separate people
one from another as a shepherd separates the sheep from the
goats, and he will put the sheep at his right hand and the goats
at the left. Then the king will say to those at his right hand,
"Come, you that are blessed by my Father, inherit the kingdom
prepared for you from the foundation of the world; for I was
hungry and you gave me food, I was thirsty and you gave
me something to drink, I was a stranger and you welcomed
me, I was naked and you gave me clothing, I was sick and you
took care of me, I was in prison and you visited me." Then the
righteous will answer him, "Lord, when was it that we saw you
hungry and gave you food, or thirsty and gave you something
to drink? And when was it that we saw you a stranger and
welcomed you, or naked and gave you clothing? And when was
it that we saw you sick or in prison and visited you?" And the
king will answer them, "Truly I tell you, just as you did it to one
of the least of these who are members of my family, you did it to
me." Matthew 25:31–40*

IN THE PARABLE OF the sheep and goats, Jesus, by way of Matthew,
offers us the clearest depiction in the Gospels of a final judgment.
Here we see a sorting between those who will inherit the kingdom
and those whose sin—their separation from God—will persist. It

has always struck me that the criterion on which the nations are sorted is not belief but practice.

There are other places and times where Jesus invites his disciples to profess his name, where he invites them to claim him as their Messiah. But nowhere in this parable does Jesus request a statement of belief. He simply asks: How did you respond to me in the face of the needs of your brothers and sisters?

When we, the church, are faced with disagreement, I suggest that we take a step back from belief and focus instead on shared practices.

This may seem to run contrary to Martin Luther's famous statement of *sola fide* ("by faith alone")—but recall that he sent up this cry in a time when the institution of the church was the jealous guardian of access to the Divine and of salvation itself. *Sola fide* was not just about the individual believer's salvation; it was also (and even primarily) about how the church makes space for people to connect with God—it was about practices.

Although belief can be and is a source of comfort, strength, and conviction for many, a narrow focus on belief can become a stumbling block. Most, if not all, of our disagreements as a church—even disagreements ostensibly about practices!—come down to differences of belief. When these differences touch on the essential dogmas of Christianity as laid out in the creeds, we do well to attend to them; when they are relevant to non-essential (which does not mean unimportant!) beliefs, we would do better to turn our attention to practice instead.

On the night that Jesus gave himself up for us, "he took a loaf of bread, and when he had given thanks, he broke it and gave it to them, saying, 'This is my body, which is given for you. Do this in remembrance of me'" (Luke 22:19) Even in the institution of the Lord's Supper, one of the special means of grace we call a sacrament, Jesus does not give us anything to believe; he gives us something to do.

Of course, belief and practice are not so easily separated. There is a chicken and egg issue here—our beliefs (hopefully!) inform our practices, and our practices reveal and form our beliefs. Belief and practice must go hand in hand. If our practices do not embody love of God and neighbor, any professed belief in the Greatest Commandment is meaningless. If our service to our neighbor is not motivated by a belief in the belovedness of all God's children, we will soon find ourselves purposeless and burned out.

But too often the church overemphasizes the role of head belief and underestimates the extent to which practices are formative, for good or ill. If we can commit to engaging in prayer, worship, and reconciliation with one another, these practices can become the refining fire that distills the most vital parts of our faith and gives us back something stronger, something truer, something we all can grab hold of.

Belief matters, but emphasis on belief above all else can be limiting and exclusive in ways some of us may never consider. Where belief refers to cognitive assent to a Christian creed, focus on belief can be unintentionally ableist, excluding those with mental and cognitive disabilities, memory loss, and dementia. It might also present challenges to people who have been traumatized by the ways in which even genuinely held beliefs have been articulated—people whose capacity to cling to the Christian faith is hampered by the ways in which that faith has done them real emotional and spiritual harm.

If we are to be bound by belief alone, we will be shattered by the barest insinuation of doubt or question; if we are bound not only by belief but also by shared practices, we make space for disagreement and growth under the secure tent of a shared Christian identity that runs deeper than our thoughts and opinions.

More than that, we make space for love. In his contemporary rendering of St. Benedict's Rule, *Always We Begin Again*, John McQuiston II said, "Love is not a belief. It is attitude and action."[44] Too often, the church has professed a belief in a God who is love, in our call to love others and to love ourselves—and then, whether knowingly or not, has preached exclusion and shame in our attitudes and actions.

The suggestion is not that we dismiss or devalue belief but that we have humility about it, that we look to have our attitudes and actions formed by love and to look there for common ground. Belief is shaped by experience; if we seek perfectly aligned beliefs as a basis for community, we are likely to end up in community only with those who look like us and whose lives have been much like ours. Humility in regards to belief is essential to making spaces for differences, not just of opinion, but of life experience, stage of spiritual journey, socioeconomic background, and so on.

As a guide for focusing on practice over belief, I offer John Wesley's Three Simple Rules: 1. Do no harm; 2. Do good; 3. Attend upon all the ordinances of God—or, as Reuben Job put it in his interpretation of these rules, "Stay in love with God."[45]

Wesley's three rules, along with practices like worship, sacraments, holy conferencing, service, and more can keep us

---

44 McQuiston, *Always We Begin Again*, xvii.

45 Job, *Three Simple Rules*, 53.

together despite differences of opinion. As John Wesley said, "Though we may not think alike, may we not love alike?"[46]

When we focus on these practices, we may find that, more often than not, we will be called to refrain from stating a belief or opinion about this or that "issue" in the life of the church. We may instead find opportunities to engage, not with an "issue," but with another child of God. We may instead find a way forward in the practice of love that we would never find in mere belief in love.

---

46 Outler, *The Works of John Wesley Vol. 2*, 82.

Discussion questions:

- What are some examples of practices in your faith community where you see people of different belief and opinion come together and find common ground?
- Where in the Bible do you find examples of practice being emphasized over belief? Where in the Bible do you find examples of belief being emphasized over practice? What does it look like to wrestle with these examples in community?
- Take some time for confession—how have you as an individual the church as a body done harm, failed to do good, or strayed from God's call? What practices might create opportunities for you and your community to adhere more closely to Wesley's Three Simple Rules?

That They Might Be One

BY: LARRY DUGGINS

I'm not praying only for them but also for those who believe in me because of their word. I pray they will be one, Father, just as you are in me and I am in you. I pray that they also will be in us, so that the world will believe that you sent me. I've given them the glory that you gave me so that they can be one just as we are one. I'm in them and you are in me so that they will be made perfectly one. Then the world will know that you sent me and that you have loved them just as you loved me.

John 17:20–23 CEB

IN MY OPINION, THIS may be the most important scripture in the Bible. This is the "why."

Jesus is with the disciples on the night of his betrayal. He has taught them, he has washed their feet—he has done all that he can do to prepare them for the night ahead and for the transformed life that will follow. He then turns to God and prays that they might be one with each other and with him just as he is one with the Father. He prays that they be brought into unity with God.

- Why did Jesus come? that they might be one with him and each other.
- Why did Jesus die? that they might be one with him and each other.
- Why was Jesus resurrected? that they might be one with him and each other.

- Why should they believe? that they might be one with him and each other.

And before we go any further, let's consider exactly who "they" are, because "they" are us. Jesus specifically says that he is praying not only for the disciples who are present with him in that time and place, but also for those who believe in him because of the word of those who were present. Those who were present were the eleven (less Judas) and the other men and women who were followers—all those who will go out and tell the gospel story after the resurrection, those who wrote the four Gospels, those who went out to make disciples of all nations. The only way those of us who are Christians today know the gospel story is through the words of those who were present with him. So, when Jesus prays this prayer, he prays for each and every person who has known, knows, or will know the gospel. He prays for all those who come to believe.

The unity that Jesus prays for is not simply an amazing and wonderful thing for us individually, it is a critical form of evangelism. Jesus prays that we might be one with him and with each other so that the world might believe that God sent Jesus and that God loves them just as God loves Jesus. As people come to believe and live into being one with Jesus and one with each other, the "world" sees and is invited to believe. A life that demonstrates the fruits of unity with Jesus and each other is a strong witness to the love of God for every individual in the world.

That Jesus prays for us to be one with him and one with each other reinforces the premise that humanity was created to live in community. If Jesus was exclusively interested in a personal relationship between God and each person, he simply would not have included the love between people in his prayer. He clearly understands that the love that people share with each other is a vital part of their fulfillment. People are only at their best when they love both God and each other. Jesus's prayer echoes his teaching of the Greatest Commandment—that we are to love God and love each other. His prayer is very specific: he prays that we will love God, that we will love each other, and that the love we share will be the same love that God shares with Jesus.

In his prayer, Jesus tells God that he has shared the "glory" that God gave Jesus with the disciples, and, by extension, with us. Like all of God's gifts, the gift of "glory" is a gift of grace, given without merit or cost. However, it is very informative to dwell for a minute on the ways that Jesus used his gift of glory. He lived a life of poverty among people of low social status. He gave extravagantly by healing, feeding, and teaching wherever he went. At great cost, he stood against those who were abusing power and authority—a stance that ultimately led him to arrest, torture, and an agonizing death. That is hardly what comes to mind when we imagine "basking in our glory."

As we work toward living into unity with Jesus and each other by living into the glory we have been given by Jesus, we may be called to set aside some of our personal agendas and comforts. Living into our glory might require us to humbly accept a stance that we are uncomfortable with, but that is necessary to build the love of Jesus and the love of others. We may be called to set aside a dispute or a strongly held opinion to preserve the witness to the world that our unity with Jesus and each other represents. Just as Jesus set aside his personal comfort and ultimately his life, we may need to set aside our pride, our ego, and even our sense of personal comfort if they conflict with the prayer of Jesus.

This stance is counter-cultural, especially in today's America. Culture teaches us to band together with those who think like we do and to vilify those who do not. We are taught to pull together all the arguments about why we are right and to seek to destroy the arguments and positions of those who disagree. We cling to idealized visions of the past—our "glory" days—and we resist or reject those who bring change. We set aside unity with Jesus and each other for unity with a much smaller band of like-minded people. We are not interested in witnessing to the outside group—we simply focus on converting them to our opinion or excluding them from our presence.

For people who strive to follow the example of Jesus in daily life and who seek to live into the unity that Jesus prays for, such group against group antagonism is simply unacceptable. The unacceptability of that divisiveness is not limited to a single camp of liberals or conservatives. The truth is that the gospel calls us to behave differently than "the world" and to value the love of God and the love of each other more highly than any other position or criterion. As we address any issue that potentially divides the Body of Christ, our first questions and unwavering guidelines should be "How does this affect my love for Jesus and my love for others? Does this bring us closer to the prayer of Jesus?"

Discussion questions:

- Do you have a scripture that you believe is the most important scripture in the Bible? How does it affect your interactions with other people?
- Have you ever considered the way that Christians behave as evangelism? Does our behavior invite others?
- How does "being one with Jesus and each other" align with your understanding of heaven? Are they the same thing?
- Is glory a responsibility?

Relational Peace

BY: LUKE LINGLE

We are fundamentally relational beings created in the image of a fundamentally relational being. Because we are relational beings we long to be in community with each other, and at times that is beautiful. At other times, in community, we cause each other harm and our communities reflect the brokenness of our world. At times community offers us the opportunity for freedom, and at times we feel captured by our communities. When our communities become places that offer less than the peace that comes through our relationship with God and each other, then we have work to do and our communities have work to do.

Often we forget that our first identity is that we are God's beloved. You are first and foremost beautifully and wonderfully made. Obviously, we hurt ourselves and others and do not always live into our identity, but it is our beginning identity nonetheless. God loves each of us and desires that we love our neighbors as ourselves, as God loves us. What happens when we forget that our identity is first and foremost as a beloved child of God? More importantly, what happens when we forget that our neighbors' identity is a beloved Child of God? What happens is that we stop listening to each other, what happens is that we look at each other through the lens of an issue or particular theological idea, what happens is that we value winning over relationship, being correct over the peace of God.

Frederick Buechner helps us think about this in a little more concretely,

> You can't really be human all by yourself, of course. You need other people to talk to and listen to and share your secrets with and laugh yourself silly with and when you really get to know each other well, even to be all to be silent together without embarrassment. That's what friends are all about.[47]

Relationship is necessary to be fully human. We need each other to reflect the image of God back to one another in tangible flesh and blood. Buechner observes that when we really get to know each other we are able to be silent together. One of the reasons that dialogue is difficult around difficult discussions is that often we don't know each other well enough to sit in silence together. We feel as though we need to fill the air with words, that we cannot trust the person we disagree with enough to stop talking. You see this with kids, when they get angry or when they disagree with a friend or sibling, they attempt to talk until the person is subdued or relents. What if our relationships call us to practice silence more than we practice sharing our own opinions, or, what if our call to relationship calls us to find places to laugh and listen more than we talk?

When we forget that we know God because we know each other, we build walls between ourselves and others. I keep a piece of the Berlin wall in my office. I was not alive when it was built but I remember when it was torn down. In college I had the opportunity to visit Berlin and to see where the wall stood. Like a good

---

47 Buechner, *Secrets in the Dark*, 305.

tourist I bought a piece of the wall. Today, the piece of the wall sits in my office to remind me what we are capable of as people as we divide ourselves from each other. The piece of the wall helps me think about walls that I put up between myself and others; walls of disagreement, walls of indifference, walls of misunderstanding, walls that make us feel better about ourselves while hurting others, walls that make us think that division is ok. I am reminded that Christ tears down walls that divide us and calls us to relationship, especially with folks we consider other. In Christ, there is not an outside or an inside; Christ's love is for all. Christ, through his life, death, and resurrection, deconstructed the dividing walls in our lives. Today, it is like there are little pieces of walls that we are trying to stack back up between ourselves and others.

The best way that I have ever seen to tear down walls is by eating together. Jesus was on to something when he shared himself and his love through bread and wine. I don't care how much you may think you are different from someone else, when we gather around table together something happens. God works through the table. At the Wild Goose Festival this year when talking about table, Ruby Sales stated, "the word inclusion presumes that one person has authority over the table." Sales reminds us that when we are followers of Christ the tables that we gather around are not our own. When we gather around table with our enemies, with folks that are not like us, with folks at whose table we would not normally gather, we are reminded that the table is first and foremost set by Christ. And all are invited to Christ's table. When we gather around the table we do not have authority or power over one another, rather we sit as guests of the prince of peace. What if we ate a meal with folks who don't have the same thoughts and ideas that we have? What if we sit around table with folks who could be perceived as enemies? This seems to me to be the call of the gospel.

Do you know someone in your community who thinks differently than you do? Would you consider having a meal with that person? What would it look like for you to break bread together? We need each other. Relationship with one another is more important than being right or wrong. Listening to each other is more important than winning a particular argument. What if going to one dinner is the beginning of walls coming down in your community?

<u>Discussion questions:</u>

- Have you shared a meal with someone with whom you disagreed?
- What are the walls that you have in your life?
- What walls have you encountered?

But What About Truth?

BY: ANDREA LINGLE

I AM SITTING IN the office I share with my husband, surrounded on three sides by books. Books that tell about the truth of Methodism, books that tell about the truth of generosity, books that tell about the truth of philosophy, economics, and the mechanics of the Hebrew language. There are commentaries, memoirs, sermon collections, and bibles. All full of truth.

But they don't all agree.

Not even all the books in the Bible agree.

So, what about the truth? Is there truth, or must we be condemned to the weakness of the relativistic truth-for-me life? Truth is difficult. It is something that is hard to define but easy to feel. We certainly do not want to be caught not telling it, and we get a creepy feeling in our gut when someone else is not telling the truth. But what if what I think is truth contradicts what you think is truth? Who is right?

Exactly.

Surrounded by all of these book, each telling a truth of its own, I am startled by the truth that every single one of them, down to the Oxford Dictionary and Thesaurus I keep, nostalgically, on my shelf, are constructed from twenty-six letters (except the Hebrew ones, but let's just let that go, for the sake of the illustration). Twenty-six letters has given us Plato, Lewis, Gladwell, and Blake, all of them different, and all of them hinting at truth.

Hinting at the Word behind the words. The Indescribable within the described.

But how do we defend that which lurks behind and within? How do speak truth if it is as broad as the universe and as unimaginable as the Higgs-Boson?

We pursue it with intense, unfettered, relentless joy. We wrestle with it until the break of day, coming away breathless, limping, and changed. We think and listen and learn and work and work and work, and, in the end, we realize that what we have been playing in was the ocean, not a puddle. We revel in the joy of being able to play in the very edge of truth, knowing that we could never hold it all.

There is a recurrent problem in my house. Picture this: the doorbell rings. A friend, whom I am expecting for dinner, is standing on my faded Welcome mat with a suitcase.

"Oh! Hi." I try very hard not to stare at the suitcase while opening the door. Then I turn with an inquisitive and acid stare to non-verbally assault my husband. Why is there a suitcase? The guest bed does not have clean sheets!! I have NOT cleaned the bathroom down there! I shriek—internally. Oh, but he hears every word.

Later after the clandestine bed change and bathroom swipe my husband and I debate the finer points of truth.

"I did tell you."

"No, you didn't. If you had told me, then I would not have been surprised."

"But, I remember telling you."

And on and so forth. If you have not had this conversation, then I am assuming you're another life form that has learned to read. Which I welcome. I do not discriminate against reading birds or wombats or lichen. But, if you happen to be human, you will have experienced the unknowable truth. Did I remember to tell you?

Personally revealing, humorous examples aside, to search for truth requires discipline, commitment, and flexibility. No one comes to a greater understanding of the truth without acknowledging that truth is greater than a single interpretation or perspective of the truth.

To facilitate a search for truth, John Wesley used what has come to be called the quadrilateral. This four-part system uses scripture, reason, tradition, and experience to explore truth. Scripture, when used as a singular pathway to truth, can be used to justify injustice. Reason alone strips life of mystery. Tradition alone discounts the evolution of the human spiritual experience. And experience alone leaves you frustrated and screaming, unable to support what you have lived to be true (he forgot to tell me she was spending the night).

Then we have to face another truth about truth. When is my rightness more important than living toward love? Sometimes truth (or your viewpoint of truth) forces you to climb a hill and die on it. If the truth you have found through your multifaceted process requires you to act, then you must. If your defense of truth lovingly protects the personhood of another, then you must defend your truth. But if not, I submit, that our responsibility is first to loving God, ourselves, and others, and not to defending truth—however it is discovered.

"Then Jesus said to the Jews who had believed in him, 'If you continue in my word, you are truly my disciples; and you will

know the truth, and the truth will make you free.'" John 8:31,32
Truth is what sets you free. Does your doctrine make you more
free, more loving, more kind? Then it might be truth. What about
your opinions? Do they make those around you free?

We have come to the table with our truths which we have
nurtured and loved because they have given us the strength and
courage to come this far. Now, shall we offer them to the Way, the
Truth, and the Life, knowing that this work of grace, this work of
faith, this work of God will go on to completion in Jesus Christ.

Discussion questions:

- What is the difference between truth and Truth?
- What would it cost you to let your truth go?
- What role does truth play in our conversations?

Bibilography

Arao, Brian and Kristi Clemens. "From Safe Spaces to Brave Spaces: A New Way to Frame Dialogue Around Diversity and Social Justice." in *The Art of Effective Facilitation,* edited by Lisa Landreman. Sterling, VA: Stylus, 2013.

Berry, Wendell. *What Matters?: Economics for a Renewed Commonwealth.* Berkeley, CA: Counterpoint, 2010.

Brown, Brené, *The Gifts of Imperfection: Let Go of Who You Think You're Supposed to Be and Embrace Who You Are.* Center City, MN; Hazelden, 2010.

Buechner, Frederick. *Secrets in the Dark: A life in Sermons.* New York: HarperCollins, 2006.

Gibbs, Robert. "Disagree, for God's Sake! Jewish Philosophy, Truth and the Future of Dialogue," Keynote Speech, from Celebration for the new Polonsky-Coexist Lectureship in Jewish Studies, on February 24, 2011, https://www.interfaith.cam.ac.uk/resources/lecturespapersandspeeches/disagreeforgodssake.

Gottman, John Mordechai and Nan Silver. *The Seven Principles for Making Marriage Work.* New York: Harmony Books, 2015.

Heath, Elaine A. and Larry Duggins. *Missional. Monastic. Mainline.* Eugene, OR: Cascade, 2014.

"How a victorious Bashar al-Assad is changing Syria," *The Economist,* June 28, 2018, https://www.economist.com/

middle-east-and-africa/2018/06/28/how-a-victorious-bashar-al-assad-is-changing-syria.

Job, Rueben P. *Three Simple Rules: A Wesleyan Way of Living.* Nashville: Abingdon Press, 2007.

McQuiston II, John. *Always We Begin Again.* New York: Morehouse Publishing, 1996.

Orr, James, Ed., "Jehonadab" from International Standard Bible Encyclopedia. "Bible Study Tools." https://www.biblestudytools.com/dictionary/jehonadab/, July 27, 2018.

Outler, Albert C. *The Works of John Wesley, Vol. 2.* Nashville: Abingdon Press, 1985.

Palmer, Parker J. "The Broken-Open Heart: Living With Faith and Hope in the Tragic Gap," A reprint from Weavings: A Journal of the Christian Spiritual Life, no XXIV:2 (March/April 2009), 10.

Palmer, Parker J. *The Courage to Teach: Exploring the Inner Landscape of a Teacher's Life,* 10th Anniversary edition. San Francisco; Jossey-Bass, 2007.

Peterson, Eugene H., Ed. *The Message Bible.* Wheaton, IL: Tyndale, 2002.

Rilke, Ranier Maria. *Letters to a Young Poet.* New York: Norton, 2004.

Shaia, Alexander John. *Heart and Mind, 2nd Ed.* Santa Fe: Journey of Quadratos, 2017.

Sowell, Thomas. *Basic Economics* New York: Basic Books, 2011.

The Common English Study Bible, Nashville: The Common English Bible, 2011.

Vanier, Jean. *Community and Growth* Mahwah, NJ: Paulist Press, 1989.

Resources

Resource list for dealing with conflict, unity, diversity, and division

Books

Crucial Conversations: Tools for Talking When Stakes Are High by Kerry Patterson (McGraw-Hill Education, 2011)

Just Listen: Discovering the Secret to Getting Through To Absolutely Anyone by Mark Goulston (AMACOM, 2015)

Mending the Divides: Creative Love in a Conflicted World by John Huckins (IVP Books, 2017)

Nonviolent Communication: Life-Changing Tools for Healthy Relationships by Marshall B. Rosenberg (PuddleDancer Press, 2015)

Peaceful Neighbor: Discovering the Countercultural Mr. Rogers by Michael G. Long (Westminster John Knox Press, 2015)

The Anatomy of Peace: Resolving the Heart of Conflict by The Arbinger Institute (Berrett-Koehler Publishers, 2015).

The Reunited States of America: How We Can Bridge the Partisan Divide by Mark Gerzon (Berrett-Koehler Publishers, 2016)

Two Views on Homosexuality, the Bible and the Church by Preston Sprinkle (Zondervan, 2016)

Conversation models

"Circles of Trust," Parker Palmer

"State of the Union," John Gottman

"Civil Conversations," OnBeing Project

Podcasts

The OnBeing Project, OnBeing.org

Specific Podcasts with:

- America Ferrera and John Paul Lederach - How Change Happens, in Generational Time
- Luis Alberto Urrea - What Borders are Really About and What We Do With them
- Rami Nashashibi and Lucas Johnson - Getting Proximate to Pain and Holding to the Power of Love
- How Friendship and Quiet Conversations Transformed a White Nationalist

The TED Radio Hour, NPRr.org/programs/ted-radio-hour/

Specific Podcasts with:

- Suzanne Simard, Wanis Kabbaj, Avi Rubin, Robin Dunbar—Networks
- Christian Picciolini, Sally Kohn, Dylan Marron, Anand Giridharadas—Why We Hate

The Work of:

John Paul Lederach

Eboo Patel

Brené Brown

Blessings, Poetry, and Words that Invite Presence

Mary Oliver

Wendell Berry

John O'Donahue, "Benedictus"

David Whyte

Avett Brothers, "No Hard Feelings"

Josh Garrels, "At the Table"